GOD MAKES THE RIVERS TO FLOW

ALSO BY EKNATH EASWARAN

*

Climbing the Blue Mountain
The Compassionate Universe
Conquest of Mind
The Constant Companion
Dialogue with Death
Gandhi the Man
The Mantram Handbook
Meditation
A More Ardent Fire
Nonviolent Soldier of Islam
Strength in the Storm
Take Your Time
The Undiscovered Country
Words to Live By
Your Life Is Your Message

*

THE BHAGAVAD GITA FOR DAILY LIVING
The End of Sorrow
Like a Thousand Suns
To Love Is to Know Me

*

CLASSICS OF INDIAN SPIRITUALITY
The Bhagavad Gita
The Dhammapada
The Upanishads

*

CLASSICS OF CHRISTIAN INSPIRATION
Love Never Faileth
Original Goodness
Seeing with the Eyes of Love

*

FOR CHILDREN
The Monkey & the Mango
Our Gandhi: Child of Fear to Man of Freedom

God Makes

the Rivers to Flow

Sacred literature

of the world

selected by

EKNATH

EASWARAN

NILGIRI PRESS

© 1982, 1991, 2003 by the Blue Mountain Center of Meditation

All rights reserved. Printed in the United States of America

Third edition, fourth printing April 2007

ISBN-13 : 978–1–58638–008–3

ISBN-10 : 1–58638–008–7

Library of Congress Control Number: 2003–103598

The Blue Mountain Center of Meditation, founded in Berkeley,

California, in 1961 by Eknath Easwaran, publishes books on how

to lead the spiritual life in the home and the community

For information please write to

Nilgiri Press, Box 256, Tomales, California 94971

On the Web at www.easwaran.org

The acknowledgments on page 323

constitute an extension of this copyright page

Table of Contents

13 *About This Book*

EKNATH EASWARAN   15 *Introduction*

PART 1   27 *At the Source*

PART 2   99 *Deep Currents*

PART 3   175 *Joining the Sea*

EKNATH EASWARAN   255 *The Message of the Scriptures*

EKNATH EASWARAN   259 *An Eight Point Program*

265 *How to Use This Book*
277 *Using Inspirational Passages
to Change Negative Thinking*
283 *Notes*
321 *Glossary*
323 *Acknowledgments*
325 *Index by Author & Source*
327 *Index by Title & First Line*

Detailed Contents

PART ONE   *At the Source*

The Upanishads   29   *Invocations*
Psalm 100   30   *Worship the Lord in Gladness*
The Isha Upanishad   31   *The Inner Ruler*
Lao Tzu   34   *Holding to the Constant*
35   *Mother of All Things*
The Chandi   36   *Hymn to the Divine Mother*
Swami Ramdas   37   *Divine Mystery*
Mahmud Shabestari   38   *The Mirror of This World*
Rabbi Abraham Isaac Kook   39   *Radiant Is the World Soul*
Kabir   40   *The Temple of the Lord*
The Shvetashvatara Upanishad   42   *The River of God*
Swami Paramananda   45   *Source of Our Existence*
46   *O Infinite Being!*
47   *Origin of All*
William Law   48   *The Deepest Part of Thy Soul*
The Chandogya Upanishad   49   *This Is the Self*
Fakhruddin Araqi   50   *The Shining Essence*
Psalm 139   52   *Lord, Thou Hast Searched Me*
Saint Anselm   54   *Teach Me*
Swami Sivananda   55   *Universal Prayer*
The Kena Upanishad   56   *That Invisible One*
Seng Ts'an   58   *Believing in Mind*
Saint Symeon the New Theologian   60   *I Know That He Reveals Himself*

Dov Baer of Mezhirech	61	*You Must Forget Yourself in Prayer*
The Katha Upanishad	62	*Perennial Joy*
Solomon ibn Gabirol	67	*The Living God*
Shantideva	68	*The Miracle of Illumination*
A Song of Sri Ramakrishna	69	*Dwell, O Mind, within Yourself*
The Tejobindu Upanishad	70	*The Shining Self*
Tukaram	72	*In Me Thou Livest*
	73	*When I Lose Myself in Thee*
The Bhagavad Gita	74	*The Illumined Man*
Baba Kuhi of Shiraz	77	*Only God I Saw*
The Dhammapada	78	*The Saint*
Meister Eckhart	79	*One with God*
The Katha Upanishad	80	*The Razor's Edge*
Jewish Liturgy	83	*Sabbath Prayer*
The Amritabindu Upanishad	84	*The Nectar of Immortality*
The Dhammapada	86	*Twin Verses*
Psalm 24	89	*The Earth Is the Lord's*
The Shvetashvatara Upanishad	90	*The Lord of Life*
Saint Clare of Assisi	93	*The Mirror of Eternity*
Swami Ramdas	94	*Such Is a Saint!*
	95	*The Central Truth*
Hazrat Inayat Khan	96	*Prayer for the Peace of the World*
	97	*Khatum*

PART TWO   *Deep Currents*

The Upanishads   101   *Invocations*

The Rig Veda   102   *United in Heart*

The Torah   103   *The Shema*

The Sutta Nipata   104   *Discourse on Good Will*

The Gospel of Saint Matthew   106   *The Sermon on the Mount*

Saint Francis of Assisi   109   *The Prayer of Saint Francis*

The Bhagavad Gita   110   *The Way of Love*

A Song of Sri Ramakrishna   113   *Dive Deep, O Mind*

114   *I Have Joined My Heart to Thee*

Elizabeth of the Trinity   115   *O My God, Trinity Whom I Adore*

Meera   116   *The Path to Your Dwelling*

117   *Come, Beloved*

118   *Life of My Life*

Mechthild of Magdeburg   119   *Lord, I Bring Thee My Treasure*

Rabi'a   120   *Night Prayer*

121   *Dawn Prayer*

Saint Francis de Sales   122   *I Am Thine, Lord*

Rabbi Eleazar Azikri   123   *Beloved of the Soul*

Thomas à Kempis   124   *The Wonderful Effect of Divine Love*

Jewish Liturgy   128   *Evening Prayer for the Sabbath*

Saint Ignatius of Loyola   129   *Just Because You Are My God*

Cardinal Newman   130   *Shine through Us*

Ansari of Herat   131   *Invocations*

Swami Omkar   138   *Prayer for Peace*

Hazrat Inayat Khan   139   *Prayer for Peace*

Saint Paul   140   *Epistle on Love*

Lao Tzu   141   *The Best*

The Dhammapada   142   *Give Up Anger*

Swami Sivananda   144   *The Way to Peace*

Lao Tzu   145   *Finding Unity*

Isaiah   146   *When You Call*

Sri Sarada Devi 147 *The Whole World Is Your Own*

Narsinha Mehta 148 *The Real Lovers of God*

Saint Patrick 149 *Christ Be with Me*

The *Ortha nan Gaidheal* 150 *Silence*

151 *This Morning I Pray*

Brother Lawrence 152 *The Practice of the Presence of God*

Rabbi Bahya ibn Pakuda 154 *Duties of the Heart*

Saint Teresa of Avila 156 *You Are Christ's Hands*

Swami Ramdas 157 *Unshakable Faith*

Hasan Kaimi Baba 158 *The Path of Love*

The Shvetashvatara Upanishad 159 *Hidden in the Heart*

Saint Thérèse of Lisieux 162 *Living on Love*

Hildegard of Bingen 165 *In Your Midst*

The Bhagavad Gita 166 *Whatever You Do*

Kabir 168 *The Unstruck Bells & Drums*

169 *The River of Love*

170 *Simple Union*

Swami Ramdas 171 *He Is Omnipresent*

Saint Teresa of Avila 172 *I Gave All My Heart*

173 *Her Heart Is Full of Joy*

PART THREE   *Joining the Sea*

The Upanishads	177	*Invocations*
The Rig Veda	178	*God Makes the Rivers to Flow*
The Book of Common Prayer	179	*I Am the Resurrection & the Life*
The *Mishkat al-Masabih*	181	*I Come to Him Running*
The Bhagavad Gita	182	*All Paths Lead to Me*
The Dhammapada	183	*The Blessing of a Well-Trained Mind*
Jewish Liturgy	184	*Mourner's Kaddish*
Solomon ibn Gabirol	185	*Adon Olam*
Native American Tradition	186	*Great Life-Giving Spirit*
Chief Yellow Lark	188	*Let Me Walk in Beauty*
The Bhagavad Gita	189	*What Is Real Never Ceases*
The Shvetashvatara Upanishad	192	*The One Appearing as Many*
Thomas à Kempis	196	*Lord That Giveth Strength*
	199	*Four Things That Bring Much Inward Peace*
The Sutta Nipata	200	*The Island*
Psalm 23	201	*The Lord Is My Shepherd*
Mahatma Gandhi	202	*The Path*
	203	*In the Midst of Darkness*
Saint Bernard of Clairvaux	204	*That Wondrous Star*
Saint Teresa of Avila	206	*Let Nothing Upset You*
Saint Francis de Sales	207	*Do Not Look with Fear*
Tukaram	208	*The One Thing Needed*
Shankara	209	*Soul of My Soul*
The Bhagavad Gita	210	*The Eternal Godhead*
The Katha Upanishad	212	*The Immortal*
Meera	215	*The Power of the Holy Name*
	216	*Even with Your Last Breath*
	217	*Singing Your Name*
Tukaram	218	*Think on His Name*
Swami Ramdas	219	*How Great Is His Name!*

Sri Chaitanya 220 *O Name, Stream Down in Moonlight*

Kabir 221 *Weaving Your Name*

A Song of Sri Ramakrishna 222 *Chant the Sweet Name of God*

Shankara 223 *Thy Holy Name*

The Chandogya Upanishad 224 *You Are That*

Saint Catherine of Genoa 226 *A Sea of Peace*

The Katha Upanishad 227 *The Tree of Eternity*

Saint Augustine 230 *Entering into Joy*

A Song of Sri Ramakrishna 231 *Thou One without a Second*

The Shvetashvatara Upanishad 232 *Love the Lord & Be Free*

Kabir 234 *The Fruit of the Tree*

The *Yoga Vasishtha* 235 *The Lamp of Wisdom*

The Dhammapada 236 *The Brahmin*

The Bhagavad Gita 241 *Be Aware of Me Always*

The Chandogya Upanishad 244 *The City of Brahman*

Jalaluddin Rumi 246 *A Garden beyond Paradise*

Mahatma Gandhi 248 *Self-Surrender*

Ravidas 249 *The City of God*

The Shvetashvatara Upanishad 250 *The Bridge to Immortality*

Eknath Easwaran 253 *Setu Prayer*

EKNATH EASWARAN

About This Book

This book is a very personal one. It itself is rather like a river, flowing through a country which is home for all of us but which very, very few have seen: the land of unity, in which all of creation is one and full of God.

There are no boundaries in this land. Those who dwell in it live in a timeless realm beyond distinctions like time, nationality, and language. So in the flow of this book, you will encounter them without regard to such distinctions: Mahatma Gandhi in the company of Saint Teresa of Avila and the Compassionate Buddha, Rabbi Abraham Isaac Kook with Thomas à Kempis, David the Psalmist with the anonymous composer of the Katha Upanishad. At the end of the book you will find brief notes about each mystic and scripture represented here, but within the book no distinction is made with regard to date, place, or religious tradition.

There is one other difference between this book and others I have seen: in addition to being a collection of inspiring spiritual literature, *God Makes the Rivers to Flow* is an instrument for transforming one's life. I have taught meditation for more than thirty years, and in this book I have collected passages for meditation which, as I can testify from my own experience, have the power to remake personality in the image of one's highest ideals. If this appeals to you, everything you need to start is here.

I have read these passages countless times over the years, yet I never tire of them. With every encounter I find deeper meaning. May you, too, find in them a river of inspiration that flows without end.

Throughout his career as a spiritual teacher, Eknath Easwaran was constantly being asked if this passage or that was appropriate for use in his method of meditation. Always he applied the criteria he had learned to trust in his own practice: the passage had to be positive, practical, universal, and inspiring, and it should come from scripture or from a man or woman whose words and life attested to the realization of the supreme reality that most of the world's great religions call God. This book began as a collection of such passages – ones he had chosen specifically for use in meditation.

As his audience grew, passages kept flowing in. In the last years of his life he was still learning of new ones and memorizing them for meditation. Many of these, approved by him for his students, have been added to this new edition. Others, contributed after his passing in 1999, have been added with the approval of his wife, Christine Easwaran.

For this edition, the passages have been organized to highlight thematic continuities. Part 1, "At the Source," features tributes to the springs of our being in the divine ground of existence. Part 2, "Deep Currents," gathers together ardent prayers of the world's great lovers of God. Part 3, "Joining the Sea," addresses the challenge of bodily death with soaring statements on immortality.

A concluding chapter, "How to Use This Book," gives recommendations for using this collection as a daily guide for harnessing the power of sacred words. This transformative potency is detailed in a brief catalog of passages that have been found particularly effective in changing negative states of mind into their positive counterparts: anger into compassion, ill will into good will, hatred into love.

Introduction

In ancient India lived a sculptor renowned for his life-sized statues of elephants. With trunks curled high, tusks thrust forward, thick legs trampling the earth, these carved beasts seemed to trumpet to the sky. One day, a king came to see these magnificent works and to commission statuary for his palace. Struck with wonder, he asked the sculptor, "What is the secret of your artistry?"

The sculptor quietly took his measure of the monarch and replied, "Great king, when, with the aid of many men, I quarry a gigantic piece of granite from the banks of the river, I have it set here in my courtyard. For a long time I do nothing but observe this block of stone and study it from every angle. I focus all my concentration on this task and won't allow anything or anybody to disturb me. At first, I see nothing but a huge and shapeless rock sitting there, meaningless, indifferent to my purposes, utterly out of place. It seems faintly resentful at having been dragged from its cool place by the rushing waters. Then, slowly, very slowly, I begin to notice something in the substance of the rock. I feel a presentiment . . . an outline, scarcely discernible, shows itself to me, though others, I suspect, would perceive nothing. I watch with an open eye and a joyous, eager heart. The outline grows stronger. Oh, yes, I can see it! An elephant is stirring in there!

"Only then do I start to work. For days flowing into weeks, I use my chisel and mallet, always clinging to my sense of that outline, which grows ever stronger. How the big fellow strains! How he yearns to be out! How he wants to live! It seems so clear now, for I know the one thing I must do: with an utter singleness of purpose, I must chip away every last bit of stone that is not elephant. What then remains will be, must be, elephant."

When I was young, my grandmother, my spiritual guide, would often tell just such a story, not only to entertain but to convey the essential truths of living. Perhaps I had asked her, as revered teachers in every religion have been asked, "What happens in the spiritual life? What are we supposed to do?"

My Granny wasn't a theologian, so she answered these questions simply with a story like that of the elephant sculptor. She was showing that we do not need to bring our real self, our higher self, into existence. It is already there. It has always been there, yearning to be out. An incomparable spark of divinity is to be found in the heart of each human being, waiting to radiate love and wisdom everywhere, because that is its nature. Amazing! This you that sometimes feels inadequate, sometimes becomes afraid or angry or depressed, that searches on and on for fulfillment, contains within itself the very fulfillment it seeks, and to a supreme degree.

Indeed, the tranquility and happiness we also feel are actually reflections of that inner reality of which we know so little. No matter what mistakes we may have made – and who hasn't made them? – this true self is ever pure and unsullied. No matter what trouble we have caused ourselves and those around us, this true self is ceaselessly loving. No matter how time passes from us and, with it, the body in which we dwell, this true self is beyond change, eternal.

Once we have become attentive to the presence of this true self, then all we really need do is resolutely chip away whatever is not divine in ourselves. I am not saying this is easy or quick. Quite the contrary; it can't be done in a week or by the weak. But the task is clearly laid out before us. By removing that which is petty and self-seeking, we bring forth all that is glorious and mindful of the whole. In this there is no loss, only gain. The chips pried away are of no consequence when compared to the magnificence of what will emerge. Can you imagine a sculptor scurrying to pick up the slivers that fall from his chisel, hoarding them, treasuring them, ignoring the statue altogether? Just so, when we get even a glimpse of the splendor of our inner being, our beloved preoccupations, predilections, and peccadillos will lose their glamour and seem utterly drab.

What remains when all that is not divine drops away is summed up in the short Sanskrit word *aroga*. The prefix *a* signifies "not a trace of"; *roga* means "illness" or "incapacity." Actually, the word loses some of its thrust in translation. In the original it connotes perfect well-being, not mere freedom from sickness. Often, you know, we say, "I'm well," when all we mean is that we haven't taken to our bed with a bottle of cough syrup, a vaporizer, and a pitcher of fruit juice – we're getting about, more or less. But perhaps we have been so far from optimum functioning for so long that we don't realize what splendid health we are capable of. This *aroga* of the spiritual life entails the complete removal of every obstacle to impeccable health, giving us a strong and energetic body, a clear mind, positive emotions, and a heart radiant with love. When we have such soundness, we are always secure, always considerate, good to be around. Our relationships flourish, and we become a boon to the earth, not a burden on it.

Every time I reflect on this, I am filled with wonder. Voices can be heard crying out that human nature is debased, that everything is meaningless, that there is nothing we can do, but the mystics of every religion testify otherwise. They assure us that in every country, under adverse circumstances and favorable, ordinary people like you and me have taken on the immense challenge of the spiritual life and made this supreme discovery. They have found out who awaits them within the body, within the mind, within the human spirit. Consider the case of Francis Bernardone, who lived in Italy in the thirteenth century. I'm focusing on him because we know that, at the beginning, he was quite an ordinary young man. By day this son of a rich cloth merchant, a bit of a popinjay, lived the life of the privileged, with its games, its position, its pleasures. By night, feeling all the vigor of youth, he strolled the streets of Assisi with his lute, crooning love ballads beneath candlelit balconies. Life was sweet, if shallow. But then the same force, the same dazzling inner light, that cast Saul of Tarsus to the earth and made him cry out, "Not I! Not I! But Christ liveth in me!" – just such a force plunges our troubadour deep within, wrenching loose all his old ways. He hears the irresistible voice of his God calling to him through a crucifix, "Francis, Francis, rebuild my church." And this meant not only the Chapel of San Damiano that lay in ruins nearby, not only the whole of the Church, but that which was closest of all – the man himself.

This tremendous turnabout in consciousness is compressed into the Prayer of Saint Francis. Whenever we repeat it, we are immersing ourselves in the spiritual wisdom of a holy lifetime. Here is the opening:

> Lord, make me an instrument of thy peace.
> Where there is hatred, let me sow love.

These lines are so deep that no one will ever fathom them. Profound, bottomless, they express the infinity of the Self. As you grow spiritually, they will mean more and more to you, without end.

But a very practical question arises here. Even if we recognize their great depth, we all know how terribly difficult it is to practice them in the constant give-and-take of life. For more than twenty years I have heard people, young and old, say that they respond to such magnificent words – that is just how they would like to be – but they don't know how to do it; it seems so far beyond their reach. In the presence of such spiritual wisdom, we feel so frail, so driven by personal concerns that we think we can never, never become like Saint Francis of Assisi.

I say to them, "There is a way." I tell them that we can change all that is selfish in us into selfless, all that is impure in us into pure, all that is unsightly into beauty. Happily, whatever our tradition, we are inheritors of straightforward spiritual practices whose power can be proved by anyone. These practices vary a bit from culture to culture, as you would expect, but essentially they are the same. Such practices are our sculptor's tools for carving away what is not-us so the real us can emerge.

Meditation is supreme among all these tested means for personal change. Nothing is so direct, so potent, so sure for releasing the divinity within us. Meditation enables us to see the lineaments of our true self and to chip away the stubbornly selfish tendencies that keep it locked within, quite, quite forgotten.

In meditation, the inspirational passage is the chisel, our concentration is the hammer, and our resolute will delivers the blows. And how the pieces fly! A very small, fine chisel edge, as you know, can wedge away huge chunks of stone. As with the other basic human tools – the lever, the pulley – we gain tremendous advantages of force. When we use our will to drive the thin edge of the passage deep into consciousness, we get the purchase to pry loose tenacious habits and negative attitudes. The passage, whether it is from the Bhagavad Gita or *The Imitation of Christ* or the Dhammapada of the Buddha, has been tempered in the flames of mystical experience, and its bite will . . . well, try it and find out for yourself just what it can do. In the end, only such personal experience persuades.

Now if we could hold an interview with a negative tendency, say, Resentment, it might say, "I don't worry! I've been safely settled in this fellow's mind for years. He takes good care of me – feeds me, dwells on me, brings me out and parades me around! All I have to do is roar and stir things up from time to time. Yes, I'm getting huge and feeling grand. And I'm proud to tell you there are even a few little rancors and vituperations running around now, spawned by yours truly!" So he may think. But I assure you that when you meditate on the glorious words of Saint Francis, you are prying him loose. You are saying in a way that goes beyond vows and good intentions that resentment is no part of you. You no longer acknowledge its right to exist. Thus, we bring ever more perceptibly into view our divine self. We use something genuine to drive out impostors that have roamed about largely through our neglect and helplessness.

To meditate and live the spiritual life we needn't drop everything and undertake an ascent of the Himalayas or Mount Athos or Cold Mountain. There are some who like to imagine themselves as pilgrims moving among the deer on high forest paths, simply clad, sipping only at pure headwaters, breathing only ethereal mountain air. Now it may sound unglamorous, but you can actually do better right where you are. Your situation may lack the grandeur of those austere and solitary peaks, but it could be a very fertile valley yielding marvelous fruit. We need people if we are to grow, and all our problems with them, properly seen, are opportunities for growth. Can you practice patience with a deer? Can you learn to forgive a redwood? But trying to live in harmony with those around you right now will bring out enormous inner toughness. Your powerful elephant will stir and come to life.

The old dispute about the relative virtues of the active way and the contemplative way is a spurious one. We require both. They are phases of a single rhythm like the pulsing of the heart, the indrawing and letting go of breath, the ebb and flow of the tides. So we go deep, deep inwards in meditation to consolidate our vital energy, and then, with greater love and wisdom, we come out into the family, the community, the world. Without action we lack opportunities for changing our old ways, and we increase our self-will rather than lessen it; without contemplation, we lack the strength to change and are blown about by our conditioning. When we meditate every day and also do our best in every situation, we walk both worthy roads, the *via contemplativa* and the *via activa*.

The passages in this book are meant for meditation. So used, they can lead us deep into our minds where the transformation of all that is selfish in us must take place. Simply reading them may console us, it may inspire us, but it cannot bring about fundamental, lasting change; meditation alone does that. Only meditation, so far as I know, can release the inner resources locked within us, and put before us problems worthy of those resources. Only meditation gives such a vital edge to life. This is maturity. This is coming into our own, as our concerns deepen and broaden, dwarfing the personal satisfactions – and worries – that once meant so much to us.

If you want to know how to use inspirational passages in meditation, please read the instructions on page 259 of this book. The basic technique, duration and pace, posture, and place are all taken up. You will also find there the outline of a complete eight-point program for spiritual living, including the use of the mantram, slowing down, and achieving one-pointed attention. For a more detailed introduction to this program of self-trans-formation, I refer you to my other books, especially *Meditation*. I would like here, though, to say a bit about the criteria I have used in selecting these particular passages.

We wouldn't use a dull chisel or one meant for wood on a piece of stone, and we should use suitable passages for medita-tion. We're not after intellectual knowledge, which helps us un-derstand and manipulate the external world. We seek spiritual wisdom, which leads to inner awareness. There, the separate strands of the external world – the people, the beasts and birds and fish, the trees and grasses, the moving waters and still, the earth itself – are brought into one great interconnected chord of life, and we find the will to live in accordance with that aware-ness. We find the will to live in perpetual love. I think you'll agree there are very few books which can ever lead us to that.

The test of suitable meditation passages is simply this: Does the passage bear the imprint of deep, personal spiritual experi-ence? Is it the statement of one who went beyond the narrow confines of past conditioning into the unfathomable recesses of the mind, there to begin the great work of transformation? This is the unmistakable stamp of authenticity. Only such precious writings can speak directly to our heart and soul. Their very words are invested with validity; we feel we are in the presence of the genuine.

The scriptures of the world's religions certainly meet this test, and so do the statements of passionate lovers of God like Saint Teresa, Kabir, Sri Ramakrishna, Ansari of Herat. And whatever lacks this validation by personal experience, however poetic or imaginative, however speculative or novel, is not suited for use in meditation.

But there is another thing to be considered: Is the passage positive, inspirational, life-affirming? We should avoid passages from whatever source that are negative, that stress our foolish errors rather than our enduring strength and wisdom, or that deprecate life in the world, which is precisely where we must do our living. Instead, let us choose passages that hold steadily before us a radiant image of the true Self we are striving to realize.

For the great principle upon which meditation rests is that we become what we meditate on. Actually, even in everyday life, we are shaped by what gains our attention and occupies our thoughts. If we spend time studying the market, checking the money rates, evaluating our portfolios, we are going to become money-people. Anyone looking sensitively into our eyes will see two big dollar signs, and we'll look out at the world through them, too. Attention can be caught in so many things: food, books, collections, travel, television. The Buddha put it succinctly: "All that we are is the result of what we have thought."

If this is true of daily life, it is even more so in meditation, which is concentration itself. In the hours spent in meditation, we are removing many years of the "what we have thought." At that time, we need the most powerful tools we can find for accomplishing the task. That is why, in selecting passages, I have aimed for the highest the human being is capable of, the most noble and elevating truths that have ever been expressed on this planet. Our petty selfishness, our vain illusions, simply must and will give way under the power of these universal principles of life, as sand castles erode before the surge of the sea.

Specifically, what happens in meditation is that we slow down the furious, fragmented activity of the mind and lead it to a measured, sustained focus on what we want to become. Under the impact of a rapidly-moving, conditioned mind, we lose our sense of freely choosing. But, as the mind slows down, we begin to gain control of it in daily life. Many habitual responses in what we eat, see, and do, and in the ways we relate to people, come under our inspection and governance. We realize that we have choices. This is profoundly liberating and takes away every trace of boredom and depression.

The passages in this collection have been drawn from many traditions, and you'll find considerable variety among them. Some are in verse, some in prose; some are from the East, some from the West; some are ancient, some quite recent; some stress love, some insight, some good works. So there are differences, yes, in tone, theme, cultural milieu, but they all have this in common: they will work.

As your meditation progresses, I encourage you to build a varied repertory of passages to guard against overfamiliarity, where the repetition can become somewhat mechanical. In this way, you can match a passage to your particular need at the time – the inspiration, the reminder, the reassurance most meaningful to you.

Nearly everyone has had some longing to be an artist and can feel some affinity with my Granny's elephant sculptor. Most of us probably spent some time at painting, writing, dancing, or music-making. Whether it has fallen away, or we still keep our hand in, we remember our touches with the great world of art, a world of beauty and harmony, of similitudes and stark contrasts, of repetition and variation, of compelling rhythms like those of the cosmos itself. We know, too, that while we can all appreciate art, only a few can create masterworks or perform them as virtuosi.

Now I wish to invite you to undertake the greatest art work of all, an undertaking which is for everyone, forever, never to be put aside, even for a single day. I speak of the purpose of life, the thing without which every other goal or achievement will lose its meaning and turn to ashes. I invite you to step back and look with your artist's eye at your own life. Consider it amorphous material, not yet deliberately crafted. Reflect upon what it is, and what it could be. Imagine how you will feel, and what those around you will lose, if it does not become what it could be. Observe that you have been given two marvelous instruments of love and service: the external instrument, this intricate network of systems that is the body; the internal, this subtle and versatile mind. Ponder the deeds they have given rise to, and the deeds they can give rise to.

And set to work. Sit for meditation, and sit again. Every day without fail, sick or well, tired or energetic, alone or with others, at home or away from home, sit for meditation, as great artists throw themselves into their creations. As you sit, you will have in hand the supreme hammer and chisel; use it to hew away all unwanted effects of your heredity, conditioning, environment, and latencies. Bring forth the noble work of art within you! My earnest wish is that one day you shall see, in all its purity, the effulgent spiritual being you really are.

GOD MAKES THE RIVERS TO FLOW

The world is the river of God,

flowing from him and flowing back to him.

— THE SHVETASHVATARA UPANISHAD

PART 1

At the Source

Invocations

1

Filled with Brahman are the things we see,
Filled with Brahman are the things we see not,
From out of Brahman floweth all that is:
From Brahman all – yet is he still the same.

O M *shanti shanti shanti*

2

May quietness descend upon my limbs,
My speech, my breath, my eyes, my ears;
May all my senses wax clear and strong.
May Brahman show himself unto me.
Never may I deny Brahman, nor Brahman me.
I with him and he with me – may we abide always together.
May there be revealed to me,
Who am devoted to Brahman,
The holy truth of the Upanishads.

O M *shanti shanti shanti*

Worship the Lord in Gladness

Raise a shout for the Lord, all the earth;
    worship the Lord in gladness;
    come into His presence with shouts of joy.
Acknowledge that the Lord is God;
    He made us and we are His,
    His people, the flock He tends.
Enter His gates with praise,
    His courts with acclamation.
Praise Him!
Bless His name!
For the Lord is good;
    His steadfast love is eternal;
    His faithfulness is for all generations.

The Inner Ruler

The Lord is enshrined in the hearts of all.
The Lord is the supreme reality.
Rejoice in him through renunciation.
Covet nothing. All belongs to the Lord.
Thus working may you live a hundred years.
Thus alone can you work in full freedom.

Those who deny the Self are born again
Blind to the Self, enveloped in darkness,
Utterly devoid of love for the Lord.

The Self is one. Ever still, the Self is
Swifter than thought, swifter than the senses.
Though motionless, he outruns all pursuit.
Without the Self, never could life exist.

The Self seems to move, but is ever still.
He seems far away, but is ever near.
He is within all, and he transcends all.

Those who see all creatures in themselves
And themselves in all creatures know no fear.
Those who see all creatures in themselves
And themselves in all creatures know no grief.
How can the multiplicity of life
Delude the one who sees its unity?

The Self is everywhere. Bright is the Self,
Indivisible, untouched by sin, wise,
Immanent and transcendent. He it is
Who holds the cosmos together.

In dark night live those
For whom the world without alone is real;
In night darker still, for whom the world within
Alone is real. The first leads to a life
Of action, the second of meditation.
But those who combine action with meditation
Go across the sea of death through action
And enter into immortality
Through the practice of meditation.
So have we heard from the wise.

In dark night live those for whom the Lord
Is transcendent only; in night darker still,
For whom he is immanent only.
But those for whom he is transcendent
And immanent cross the sea of death
With the immanent and enter into
Immortality with the transcendent.
So have we heard from the wise.

The face of truth is hidden by your orb
Of gold, O sun. May you remove the orb
So that I, who adore the true, may see
The glory of truth. O nourishing sun,
Solitary traveler, controller,
Source of life for all creatures, spread your light,
And subdue your dazzling splendor
So that I may see your blessed Self.
Even that very Self am I!

May my life merge in the Immortal
When my body is reduced to ashes!
O mind, meditate on the eternal
Brahman. Remember the deeds of the past.
Remember, O mind, remember.

O God of fire, lead us by the good path
To eternal joy. You know all our deeds.
Deliver us from evil, we that bow
And pray again and again.

LAO TZU

Holding to the Constant

Break into the peace within,
Hold attention in stillness,
And in the world outside
You will ably master the ten thousand things.

All things rise and flourish
Then go back to their roots.
Seeing this return brings true rest,
Where you discover who you really are.
Knowing who you are, you will find the constant.
Those who lack harmony with the constant court danger,
But those who have it gain new vision.

They act with compassion;
    within themselves, they can find room for everything.
Having room, they rule themselves and lead others wisely.
Being wise, they live in accordance
    with the nature of things.
Emptied of self and one with nature,
They become filled with the Tao.
The Tao endures forever.
For those who have attained harmony with the Tao
    will never lose it,
Even if their bodies die.

∽

Mother of All Things

The universe had a beginning
Called the Mother of All Things.
Once you have found the Mother
You can know her children.
Having known the children,
Hold tightly to the Mother.
Your whole life will be preserved from peril.

Open up the openings,
Multiply your affairs,
Your whole life will become a burden.

Those who see the small are called clear-headed;
Those who hold to gentleness are called strong.

Use the light.
Come home to your true nature.
Don't cause yourself injury:
This is known as seizing truth.

THE CHANDI

Hymn to the Divine Mother

O thou the giver of all blessings,
O thou the doer of all good,
O thou the fulfiller of all desires,
O thou the giver of refuge –
Our salutations to thee, O Mother Divine.

O thou Eternal Mother,
Thou hast the power to create, to preserve, and to dissolve.
Thou the dwelling-place and embodiment of the three gunas –
Our salutations to thee, O Mother Divine.

O thou the savior of all who take refuge in thee,
The lowly and the distressed –
O Mother Divine, we salute thee,
Who takest away the sufferings of all.

Divine Mystery

O Mother Divine!
Thou hast filled my entire being
With Thy power all-pervading
And hast made me Thy child –
A child born of Thy joy and Thy love –
A child ever aware of Thy glory,
Basking in the rare light of Thy grace.
How wondrous art Thou! from whom cometh forth
The splendor of sun, moon, fire, stars.
Thou sporteth, O Mother, as all the worlds,
Each being and thing is Thyself in Thy myriad forms.
How can I describe Thee – O Divine Mystery!
Thou hast held me in Thy arms;
I am free, playful, and buoyant
Under Thy assuring glance and tender care.

MAHMUD SHABESTARI

The Mirror of This World

Every particle of the world is a mirror,
In each atom lies the blazing light
   of a thousand suns.
Cleave the heart of a raindrop,
   a hundred pure oceans will flow forth.
Look closely at a grain of sand,
   The seed of a thousand beings can be seen.
The foot of an ant is larger than an elephant;
In essence, a drop of water
   is no different than the Nile.
In the heart of a barley-corn
   lies the fruit of a hundred harvests;
Within the pulp of a millet seed
   an entire universe can be found.
In the wing of a fly, an ocean of wonder;
In the pupil of the eye, an endless heaven.
Though the inner chamber of the heart is small,
   the Lord of both worlds
   gladly makes his home there.

❧

Radiant Is the World Soul

Radiant is the world soul,
Full of splendor and beauty,
Full of life,
Of souls hidden,
Of treasures of the holy spirit,
Of fountains of strength,
Of greatness and beauty.
Proudly I ascend
Toward the heights of the world soul
That gives life to the universe.
How majestic the vision –
Come, enjoy,
Come, find peace,
Embrace delight,
Taste and see that God is good.
Why spend your substance on what does not nourish
And your labor on what cannot satisfy?
Listen to me, and you will enjoy what is good,
And find delight in what is truly precious.

The Temple of the Lord

As oil is in the oil seed,
And fire is in the flint,
So is the Lord within thee, unrevealed.
Follow thy Master's simple and true instructions,
Keep vigil strict at midnight and so find Him.

As fragrance is within the flower's blossom,
So is the Lord within thee, unrevealed.
But as the musk-deer searches for musk in forest grass,
So does man search for Him outside
And finds Him not.

As the pupil is within the eye itself,
So is the Lord within thy body;
But fools know not this simple fact,
And search for Him elsewhere.

As air pervades all space,
But none can see it,
So does the Lord pervade the body;
But He remains to each one unrevealed,
Since the lodestone of the heart is not attached to Him.

O man, the object of supremest value,
For which you search throughout the world,
    is here within you,
But the veil of Illusion ever separates you from Him.
Tear the veil boldly asunder and you will find Him.

My Lord is living in each human being;
There is no bridal bed without the Bridegroom.
But blessed is the body
In which He reveals Himself.

As fragrance is in the flower,
So is the Lord within thee.
But He reveals Himself in His beloved Saints;
That is all you need to know. Go forth and meet them.

The River of God

Spiritual aspirants ask their teacher:
What is the cause of the cosmos? Is it Brahman?
From where do we come? By what live?
Where shall we find peace at last?
What power governs the duality
Of pleasure and pain by which we are driven?

Time, nature, necessity, accident,
Elements, energy, intelligence –
None of these can be the first cause.
They are effects, whose only purpose is
To help the self to rise above pleasure and pain.

In the depths of meditation, sages
Saw within themselves the Lord of Love,
Who dwells in the heart of every creature.
Deep in the hearts of all he dwells, hidden
Behind the gunas of law, energy,
And inertia. He is One. He it is
Who rules over time, space, and causality.

The world is the wheel of God, turning round
And round with all living creatures upon
The wheel. The world is the river of God,
Flowing from him and flowing back to him.

On this ever-revolving wheel of life
The individual self goes round and round
Through life after life, believing itself
To be a separate creature, until
It sees its identity with the Lord
Of Love and attains immortality
In the indivisible Whole.

He is the eternal reality, sing
The scriptures, and the ground of existence.
They who perceive him in every creature
Merge in him and are released from the wheel
Of birth and death.

The Lord of Love holds in his hand the world,
Composed of the changing and the changeless,
The manifest and the unmanifest.
The individual self, not yet aware
Of the Lord, goes after pleasure, to become
Bound more and more. When it sees the Lord,
There comes the end of its bondage.

Conscious spirit and unconscious matter
Both have existed since the dawn of time,
With maya appearing to connect them,
Misrepresenting joy as outside us.
When all these three are seen as one, the Self
Reveals its universal form and serves
As an instrument of the divine will.

All is change in the world of the senses,
But changeless is the supreme Lord of Love.
Meditate on him, be absorbed in him,
Wake up from this dream of separateness.

Know God and all fetters will fall away.
No longer identifying yourself
With the body, go beyond birth and death.
All your desires will be fulfilled in him
Who is One without a second.

Know him to be enshrined within your heart
Always. Truly there is nothing more
To know in life. Meditate and realize
The world is filled with the presence of God.

Fire is not seen until one firestick rubs
Against another, though the fire remains
Hidden in the firestick. So does the Lord
Remain hidden in the body until
He is revealed through the mystic mantram.

Let your body be the lower firestick;
Let the mantram be the upper. Rub them
Against each other in meditation
And realize the Lord.

Like oil in sesame seeds, like butter
In cream, like water in springs, like fire
In a firestick, so dwells the Lord of Love,
The Self, in the very depths of consciousness.
Realize him through truth and meditation.

The Self is hidden in the hearts of all,
As butter lies hidden in cream. Realize
The Self in the depths of meditation,
The Lord of Love, supreme reality,
Who is the goal of all knowledge.

This is the highest mystical teaching;
This is the highest mystical teaching.

Source of Our Existence

O Thou Compassionate, All-loving Spirit!
Thou art the sustaining power of our life.
Thou art the unalterable source of our existence.
Thou art eternally abiding within us.
Thou art above us and below us; Thou art before us and behind us;
    Thou art all about us.
Unfold our understanding that we may comprehend Thy vastness.
Reveal unto us Thy Divine Grace that we may be sustained by
    the knowledge of Thy Presence within us.
Fill our hearts with Thy holy inspiration that we may follow
    Thy path with unwavering faith and undaunted courage.
Consecrate and sanctify our life.
Make us like little children, gentle, sweet and free from all blemish.
Fill our whole being with Thy Divine Light that we may know
    all things in that Light.
Bestow upon us the gift of true vision that we may love
    in Thy Love and live in Thy Life.
Teach us how we may partake of Thy blessedness.
We come to Thee with humility and devotion.
Grant unto us Thy abiding protection and surround us
    with Thine all-enfolding peace.

O Infinite Being!

O Infinite Being! O Supreme Lord!
Teach us how to pray and how to meditate.

Make our thoughts so one-pointed, deep and unwavering
  that they may penetrate the inner depths of our being
  and perceive Thee.

Lift our mind to that plane where there is no heaviness,
  where there is no darkness, but only illumination and bliss.

Lead us from delusion to the Light of Wisdom.

Grant that we may feel Thy Divine Presence within us;
That our soul may awaken from the sense-slumber of unreality
  and be ready to hear Thy call;
That our heart may be full of tolerance and compassion;
That peace and tranquility may pervade our whole being.

May Thy peace and blessing abide with us and protect us
  from all unworthy thoughts and actions.

Peace! Peace! Peace be upon all living beings.

Origin of All

O Supreme Deity, Mother of the moving
and unmoving, come, manifest Thyself to us.

Thou art nameless, formless, but Thou comest when
there is the genuine call. That call Thou answerest.

Thou art the Giver of all blessing, of all understanding.
Thou art the origin of all. Thou art all.

Through Thy grace the dumb become eloquent,
the lame run.

Thou art the only Doer.
Give us strength, purity, and inspiration.
Teach us how to surrender to Thee, how to call Thee.

Thou art the Supreme Lord.
Thou art the Source of all Bliss.

Manifest Thyself to us. Come to us.
Make Thy Divine Presence felt in our hearts.

Grant unto us Thy peace and blessing.

The Deepest Part of Thy Soul

Though God be everywhere present,
    yet He is only present to thee
    in the deepest and most central part of thy soul.
Thy natural senses cannot possess God
    or unite thee to Him; nay, thy inward faculties
    of understanding, will, and memory can only
    reach after God, but cannot be the place
    of His habitation in thee.

But there is a root or depth in thee
    from whence all these faculties come forth,
    as lines from a centre or as branches from
    the body of a tree.
This depth is called the Centre, the Fund
    or Bottom of the soul.
This depth is the unity, the eternity, I had almost said
    the infinity of thy soul; for it is so infinite
    that nothing can satisfy it or give it any rest
    but the infinity of God.

❧

This Is the Self

This universe comes forth from Brahman, exists in Brahman, and will return to Brahman. Verily all is Brahman.

A man is what his deep desire is. It is his deep desire in this life that shapes his life to come. So let him direct his deep desire to realize the Self.

The Self, who can be realized by the pure in heart, who is life, light, truth, space, who gives rise to all works, all desires, all odors, all tastes, who is beyond words, who is joy abiding – this is the Self dwelling in my heart.

Smaller than a grain of rice, smaller than a grain of barley, smaller than a mustard seed, smaller than a grain of millet, smaller even than the kernel of a grain of millet is the Self. This is the Self dwelling in my heart, greater than the earth, greater than the sky, greater than all the worlds.

This Self who gives rise to all works, all desires, all odors, all tastes, who pervades the universe, who is beyond words, who is joy abiding, who is ever present in my heart, is Brahman indeed. To him I shall attain when my ego dies.

❧

The Shining Essence

I look into the mirror and see my own beauty;
I see the truth of the universe revealing itself as me.

I rise in the sky as the morning Sun, do not be surprised,
Every particle of creation is me alone.

What are the holy spirits? my essence revealed.
And the human body? the vessel of my own form.

What is the ocean that encircles the world?
A drop of my abundant Grace;
And the purest light that fills every soul?
A spark of my own illumination.

I am Light itself, reflected in the heart of everyone;
I am the treasure of the Divine Name,
    the shining Essence of all things.

I am every light that shines,
Every ray that illumines the world.

From the highest heavens to the bedrock of the earth
All is but a shadow of my splendor.

If I dropped the veil covering my true essence
The world would be gone – lost in a brilliant light.

What is the water that gives eternal life?
A drop of my divine nectar.
And the breath that brings the dead back to life?
A puff of my breath, the breath of all life.

Lord, Thou Hast Searched Me

O Lord, Thou hast searched me, and known me.

Thou knowest my downsitting and mine uprising,
    Thou understandest my thought afar off.

Thou measurest my going about and my lying down,
    and art acquainted with all my ways.

For there is not a word in my tongue, but, lo, O Lord,
    Thou knowest it altogether.

Thou hast hemmed me in behind and before,
    and laid Thy hand upon me.

Such knowledge is too wonderful for me;
    too high, I cannot attain unto it.

Whither shall I go from Thy spirit?
    Or whither shall I flee from Thy presence?

If I ascend up into heaven, Thou art there;
    if I make my bed in the netherworld, behold,
Thou art there.

If I take the wings of the morning,
    and dwell in the uttermost parts of the sea;
Even there would Thy hand lead me,
    and Thy right hand would hold me.

And if I say: "Surely the darkness shall envelop me,
    and the light about me shall be night,"

Even the darkness is not too dark for Thee,
    but the night shineth as the day;
    the darkness is even as the light.

For Thou hast made my reins;
    Thou hast knit me together in my mother's womb.

I will give thanks unto Thee,
    for I am fearfully and wonderfully made;
    wonderful are Thy works,
    and that my soul knoweth right well.

My frame was not hidden from Thee
    when I was made in secret
    and curiously wrought in the lowest parts of the earth.

Thine eyes did see mine unformed substance,
    and in Thy book they were all written –
    even the days that were fashioned
    when as yet there was none of them.

How weighty also are Thy thoughts unto me, O God!
    How great is the sum of them!

If I would count them,
    they are more in number than the sand;
Were I to come to the end of them,
    I would still be with Thee.

Search me, O God, and know my heart,
    try me, and know my thoughts;
And see if there be any way in me that is grievous,
    and lead me in the way everlasting.

∾

Teach Me

Be it mine to look up to thy light, even from afar, even from the depths. Teach me to seek thee, and reveal thyself to me when I seek thee, for I cannot seek thee except thou teach me, nor find thee, except thou reveal thyself. Let me seek thee in longing, let me long for thee in seeking; let me find thee in love, and love thee in finding.

Lord, I acknowledge and I thank thee that thou hast created me in this thine image, in order that I may be mindful of thee, may conceive of thee, and love thee; but that image has been so consumed and wasted away by vices, and obscured by the smoke of wrong-doing, that it cannot achieve that for which it was made, except thou renew it, and create it anew.

I do not endeavor, O Lord, to penetrate thy sublimity, for in no wise do I compare my understanding with that; but I long to understand in some degree thy truth, which my heart believes and loves. For I do not seek to understand that I may believe, but I believe in order to understand. For this also I believe: that unless I believed I should not understand.

Universal Prayer

O adorable Lord of mercy and love,
Salutations and prostrations unto Thee.
Thou art omnipotent, omnipresent, omniscient;
Thou art Satchidananda, Truth, Knowledge, and Bliss;
Thou art the Indweller of all beings.

Grant us an understanding heart,
Equal vision, balanced mind,
Faith, devotion, and wisdom.
Grant us inner spiritual strength
To resist temptations and to control the mind.
Free us from egoism, lust, greed, and hatred,
Fill our hearts with divine virtues.

Let us behold Thee in all these names and forms,
Let us serve Thee in all these names and forms,
Let us ever remember Thee,
Let us ever sing Thy glories,
Let Thy name be ever on our lips,
Let us abide in Thee for ever and ever.

That Invisible One

The student inquires: "Who makes my mind think?
Who fills my body with vitality?
Who causes my tongue to speak? Who is that
Invisible One who sees through my eyes
And hears through my ears?"

The teacher replies: "The Self is the ear of the ear,
The eye of the eye, the mind of the mind,
The word of words, and the life of life.
Rising above the senses and the mind
And renouncing separate existence,
The wise realize the deathless Self.

"Him our eyes cannot see, nor words express;
He cannot be grasped even by our mind.
We do not know, we cannot understand,
Because he is different from the known
And he is different from the unknown.
Thus have we heard from the illumined ones.

"That which makes the tongue speak, but cannot be
Spoken by the tongue, know that as the Self.
This Self is not someone other than you.

"That which makes the mind think, but cannot be
Thought by the mind, that is the Self indeed.
This Self is not someone other than you.

"That which makes the eye see, but cannot be
Seen by the eye, that is the Self indeed.
This Self is not someone other than you.

"That which makes the ear hear, but cannot be
Heard by the ear, that is the Self indeed.
This Self is not someone other than you.

"That which makes you draw breath, but cannot be
Drawn by your breath, that is the Self indeed.
This Self is not someone other than you."

∾

Believing in Mind

The great Way has no impediments;
It does not pick and choose.
When you abandon attachment and aversion
You see it plainly.
Make a thousandth of an inch distinction,
Heaven and earth swing apart.
If you want it to appear before your eyes,
Cherish neither *for* nor *against*.

To compare what you like with what you dislike,
That is the disease of the mind.
You pass over the hidden meaning;
Peace of mind is needlessly troubled.

It is round and perfect like vast space,
Lacks nothing, never overflows.
Only because we take and reject
Do we lose the means to know its Suchness.

Don't get tangled in outward desire
Or get caught within yourself.
Once you plant deep the longing for peace
Confusion leaves of itself.

Return to the root and find meaning;
Follow sense objects, you lose the goal.
Just one instant of inner enlightenment
Will take you far beyond the emptiness of the world.

Selfish attachment forgets all limits;
It always leads down evil roads.
When you let go of it, things happen of themselves;
The substance neither goes nor abides.

If the eye does not sleep
All dreams will naturally stop.
If the mind does not differentiate
All things are of one Suchness.

When you fathom the realm of Suchness
You instantly forget all selfish desire.
Having seen ten thousand things as one
You return to your natural state.

Without meditation
Consciousness and feeling are hard to grasp.
In the realm of Suchness
There is neither self nor other.

In the one, there is the all.
In the all, there is the one.
If you know this,
You will never worry about being incomplete.

If belief and mind are made the same
And there is no division between belief and mind
The road of words comes to an end,
Beyond present and future.

I Know That He Reveals Himself

I sit alone apart from all the world
    and see before me Him who transcends the world.
I see Him and He sees me;
I love Him and I believe that He loves me;
I am nourished and satisfied only with His vision.
United with Him I go beyond heaven.
All this I know beyond any doubt,
    but where my body is I do not know.

I know that He who is immovable descends;
I know that He who is invisible appears to me;
I know that He who transcends all creation
    takes me into Himself and hides me in His arms
    apart from all the world;
and then I, small and mortal in this world,
    I see the Creator of the world within me
and know that I can never die
    because I have eternal life
    and all of life wells up in me.
He is in my heart, He is in heaven;
    both here and there He reveals Himself to me
    in equal glory.

You Must Forget Yourself in Prayer

You must forget yourself in prayer.
Think of yourself as nothing
    and pray only for the sake of God.
In such prayer you may come to transcend time,
    entering the highest realms
    of the World of Thought.
There all things are as one;
Distinctions between "life" and "death,"
    "land" and "sea,"
    have lost their meaning.
But none of this can happen
    as long as you remain attached
    to the reality of the material world.
Here you are bound to the distinctions
    between good and evil
    that emerge only in the lower realms of God.
How can one who remains attached to his own self
    go beyond time to the world where all is one?

Perennial Joy

THE KING OF DEATH:

The joy of the spirit ever abides,
But not what seems pleasant to the senses.
Both these, differing in their purpose, prompt us
To action. All is well for those who choose
The joy of the spirit, but they miss
The goal of life who prefer the pleasant.
Perennial joy or passing pleasure?
This is the choice one is to make always.
The wise recognize this, but not
The ignorant. The first welcome what leads to joy
Abiding, even though painful at the time.
The latter run, goaded by their senses,
After what seems immediate pleasure.

Well have you renounced these passing pleasures
So dear to the senses, Nachiketa,
And turned your back on the way of the world
Which makes mankind forget the goal of life.

Far apart are wisdom and ignorance:
The first leads one to Self-realization;
The second makes one more and more
Estranged from one's real Self. I regard you,
Nachiketa, as worthy of instruction,
For passing pleasures tempt you not at all.

Ignorant of their ignorance yet wise
In their own esteem, deluded people
Proud of their vain learning go round and round
Like the blind led by the blind. Far beyond
Their eyes, hypnotized by the world of sense,
Opens the way to immortality.
"I am my body; when my body dies,
I die." Living in this superstition they fall,
Life after life, under my sway.

It is but few who hear about the Self.
Fewer still dedicate their lives to its
Realization. Wonderful is the one
Who speaks of the Self. Rare are they
Who make it the supreme goal of their life.
Blessed are they who, through an illumined
Teacher, attain to Self-realization.
The truth of the Self cannot come through one
Who has not realized that he is the Self.
The intellect can never reach the Self,
Beyond its duality of subject
And object. He who sees himself in all
And all in him helps one through spiritual
Osmosis to realize the Self oneself.
This awakening you have known comes not
Through logic and scholarship, but from
Close association with a realized teacher.
Wise are you, Nachiketa, because you
Seek the Self eternal. May we have more
Seekers like you!

NACHIKETA:

I know that earthly treasures are transient,
And never can I reach the Eternal
Through them. Hence have I renounced
All the desires of Nachiketa for earthly treasures
To win the Eternal through your instruction.

I spread before your eyes, Nachiketa,
The fulfillment of all worldly desires:
Power to dominate the earth, delights
Celestial gained through religious rites, and
Miraculous powers beyond time and space.
These with will and wisdom have you renounced.

The wise, realizing through meditation
The timeless Self, beyond all perception,
Hidden in the cave of the heart,
Leave pain and pleasure far behind.
Those who know that they are neither body
Nor mind but the immemorial Self,
The divine principle of existence,
Find the source of all joy and live in joy
Abiding. I see the gates of joy
Are opening for you, Nachiketa.

NACHIKETA:

Teach me of That you see as beyond right
And wrong, cause and effect, past and future.

THE KING OF DEATH:

I will give you the Word all the scriptures
Glorify, all spiritual disciplines
Express, to attain which aspirants lead
A life of sense-restraint and self-naughting.
It is OM. This symbol of the Godhead
Is the highest. Realizing it, one finds
Complete fulfillment of all one's longings.
It is the greatest support to all seekers.
When OM reverberates unceasingly
Within one's heart, that one is indeed blessed
And greatly loved as one who is the Self.

The all-knowing Self was never born,
Nor will it die. Beyond cause and effect,
This Self is eternal and immutable.
When the body dies, the Self does not die.
If the slayer believes that he can kill
And the slain believes that he can be killed,
Neither knows the truth. The eternal Self
Slays not, nor is ever slain.

Hidden in the heart of every creature
Exists the Self, subtler than the subtlest,
Greater than the greatest. They go beyond
All sorrow who extinguish their self-will
And behold the glory of the Self
Through the grace of the Lord of Love.

Though one sits in meditation in a
Particular place, the Self within can
Exercise its influence far away.
Though still, it moves everything everywhere.

When the wise realize the Self, formless
In the midst of forms, changeless in the midst
Of change, omnipresent and supreme,
They go beyond all sorrow.

The Self cannot be known through the study
Of the scriptures, nor through the intellect,
Nor through hearing discourses about it.
It can be attained only by those
Whom the Self chooses. Verily unto them
Does the Self reveal itself.

The Self cannot be known by anyone
Who desists not from unrighteous ways,
Controls not the senses, stills not the mind,
And practices not meditation.

None else can know the omnipresent Self,
Whose glory sweeps away the rituals of
The priest and the prowess of the warrior
And puts death itself to death.

The Living God

Bow down before God, my precious thinking soul,
and make haste to worship Him with reverence.

Night and day think only of your everlasting world.

Why should you chase after vanity and emptiness?

As long as you live, you are akin to the living God:
just as He is invisible, so are you.

Since your Creator is pure and flawless,
know that you too are pure and perfect.

The Mighty One upholds the heavens on His arm,
as you uphold the mute body.

My soul, let your songs come before your Rock,
who does not lay your form in the dust.

My innermost heart, bless your Rock always,
whose name is praised by everything that has breath.

The Miracle of Illumination

As a blind man feels when he finds a pearl
  in a dustbin, so am I amazed by the miracle
  of Bodhi rising in my consciousness.
It is the nectar of immortality that delivers us from death,
The treasure that lifts us above poverty into
  the wealth of giving to life,
The tree that gives shade to us when we roam about
  scorched by life,
The bridge that takes us across the stormy river of life,
The cool moon of compassion that calms our mind
  when it is agitated,
The sun that dispels darkness,
The butter made from the milk of kindness
  by churning it with the dharma.
It is a feast of joy to which all are invited.

Dwell, O Mind, Within Yourself

Dwell, O mind, within yourself;
Enter no other's home.
If you but seek there, you will find
All you are searching for.

God, the true Philosopher's Stone,
Who answers every prayer,
Lies hidden deep within your heart,
The richest gem of all.

How many pearls and precious stones
Are scattered all about
The outer court that lies before
The chamber of your heart!

The Shining Self

Let us meditate on the shining Self,
Changeless, underlying the world of change,
And realized in the heart in samadhi.

Hard to reach is the supreme goal of life,
Hard to describe and hard to abide in.
They alone attain samadhi who have
Mastered their senses and are free from anger,
Free from self-will and from likes and dislikes,
Without selfish bonds to people and things.

They alone attain samadhi who are
Prepared to face challenge after challenge
In the three stages of meditation.
Under an illumined teacher's guidance
They become united with the Lord of Love,
Called Vishnu, who is present everywhere.
Though the three gunas emanate from him,
He is infinite and invisible.
Though all the galaxies emerge from him,
He is without form and unconditioned.

To be united with the Lord of Love
Is to be freed from all conditioning.
This is the state of Self-realization,
Far beyond the reach of words and thoughts.
To be united with the Lord of Love,
Imperishable, changeless, beyond cause
And effect, is to find infinite joy.
Brahman is beyond all duality,
Beyond the reach of thinker and of thought.

Let us meditate on the shining Self,
The ultimate reality, who is
Realized by the sages in samadhi.

Brahman cannot be realized by those
Who are subject to greed, fear, and anger.
Brahman cannot be realized by those
Who are subject to the pride of name and fame
Or to the vanity of scholarship.
Brahman cannot be realized by those
Who are enmeshed in life's duality.

But to all those who pierce this duality,
Whose hearts are given to the Lord of Love,
He gives himself through his infinite grace;
He gives himself through his infinite grace.

In Me Thou Livest

Take, Lord, unto Thyself
My sense of self; and let it vanish utterly.

Take, Lord, my life,
Live Thou my life through me.

I live no longer, Lord,
But in me now
Thou livest.

Aye, between Thee and me, my God,
There is no longer room for "I" and "mine."

When I Lose Myself in Thee

When thus I lose myself in Thee, my God,
Then do I see, and know,
That all Thy universe reveals Thy beauty,
All living beings, and all lifeless things,
Exist through Thee.

This whole vast world is but the form
In which Thou showest us Thyself,
Is but the voice
In which Thyself Thou speakest unto us.

What need of words?
Come, Master, come,
And fill me wholly with Thyself.

The Illumined Man

ARJUNA:

Tell me of the man who lives in wisdom,
Ever aware of the Self, O Krishna;
How does he talk, how sit, how move about?

SRI KRISHNA:

He lives in wisdom
Who sees himself in all and all in him,
Whose love for the Lord of Love has consumed
Every selfish desire and sense craving
Tormenting the heart. Not agitated
By grief nor hankering after pleasure,
He lives free from lust and fear and anger.
Fettered no more by selfish attachments,
He is not elated by good fortune
Nor depressed by bad. Such is the seer.

Even as a tortoise draws in its limbs
The sage can draw in his senses at will.
An aspirant abstains from sense-pleasures,
But he still craves for them. These cravings all
Disappear when he sees the Lord of Love.

For even of one who treads the path
The stormy senses can sweep off the mind.
But he lives in wisdom who subdues them,
And keeps his mind ever absorbed in me.

When you keep thinking about sense-objects,
Attachment comes. Attachment breeds desire,
The lust of possession which, when thwarted,
Burns to anger. Anger clouds the judgment
And robs you of the power to learn from past mistakes.
Lost is the discriminative faculty,
And your life is utter waste.

But when you move amidst the world of sense
From both attachment and aversion freed,
There comes the peace in which all sorrows end,
And you live in the wisdom of the Self.

The disunited mind is far from wise;
How can it meditate? How be at peace?
When you know no peace, how can you know joy?
When you let your mind follow the Siren call
Of the senses, they carry away
Your better judgment as a cyclone drives a boat
Off the charted course to its doom.

Use your mighty arms to free the senses
From attachment and aversion alike,
And live in the full wisdom of the Self.
Such a sage awakes to light in the night
Of all creatures. Wherein they are awake
Is the night of ignorance to the sage.

As the rivers flow into the ocean
But cannot make the vast ocean o'erflow,
So flow the magic streams of the sense-world
Into the sea of peace that is the sage.

He is forever free who has broken out
Of the ego-cage of I and mine
To be united with the Lord of Love.
This is the supreme state. Attain thou this
And pass from death to immortality.

BABA KUHI OF SHIRAZ
Only God I Saw

In the market, in the cloister – only God I saw.
In the valley and on the mountain – only God I saw.

Him I have seen beside me oft in tribulation;
In favor and in fortune – only God I saw.

In prayer and fasting, in praise and contemplation,
In the religion of the Prophet – only God I saw.

Neither soul nor body, accident nor substance,
Qualities nor causes – only God I saw.

I oped mine eyes and by the light of his face around me
In all the eye discovered – only God I saw.

Like a candle I was melting in his fire:
Amidst the flames outflashing – only God I saw.

Myself with mine own eyes I saw most clearly,
But when I looked with God's eyes – only God I saw.

I passed away into nothingness, I vanished,
And lo, I was the All-living – only God I saw.

❧

The Saint

He has completed his voyage; he has gone beyond sorrow. The fetters of life have fallen from him, and he lives in full freedom.

The thoughtful strive always. They have no fixed abode, but leave home like swans from their lake.

Like the flight of birds in the sky, it is hard to follow the path of the selfless. They have no possessions, but live on alms in a world of freedom. Like the flight of birds in the sky, it is hard to follow their path. With their senses under control, temperate in eating, they know the meaning of freedom.

Even the gods envy the saints, whose senses obey them like well-trained horses and who are free from pride. Patient like the earth, they stand like a threshold. They are pure like a lake without mud, and free from the cycle of birth and death.

Wisdom has stilled their minds, and their thoughts, words, and deeds are filled with peace. Freed from illusion and from personal ties, they have renounced the world of appearance to find reality. Thus have they reached the highest.

They make holy wherever they dwell, in village or forest, on land or at sea. With their senses at peace and minds full of joy, they make the forests holy.

One with God

Whoever has God in mind,
simply and solely God, in all things,
such a man carries God with him into all his works
and into all places,
and God alone does all his works.
He seeks nothing but God,
nothing seems good to him but God.
He becomes one with God in every thought.
Just as no multiplicity can dissipate God,
so nothing can dissipate this man or make him multiple.

The Razor's Edge

In the secret cave of the heart, two are
Seated by life's fountain. The separate ego
Drinks of the sweet and bitter stuff,
Liking the sweet, disliking the bitter,
While the supreme Self drinks sweet and bitter
Neither liking this nor disliking that.
The ego gropes in darkness, while the Self
Lives in light. So declare the illumined sages,
And the householders who worship
The sacred fire in the name of the Lord.

May we light the fire of Nachiketa
That burns out the ego, and enables us
To pass from fearful fragmentation
To fearless fullness in the changeless Whole.

Know the Self as lord of the chariot,
The body as the chariot itself,
The discriminating intellect as
The charioteer, and the mind as the reins.
The senses, say the wise, are the horses;
Selfish desires are the roads they travel.
When the Self is confused with the body,
Mind, and senses, they point out, it seems
To enjoy pleasure and suffer sorrow.

When a person lacks discrimination
And his mind is undisciplined, his senses
Run hither and thither like wild horses.
But they obey the rein like trained horses
When a person has discrimination
And the mind is one-pointed. Those who lack
Discrimination, with little control
Over their thoughts and far from pure,
Reach not the pure state of immortality
But wander from death to death; while those
Who have discrimination, with a still mind
And a pure heart, reach journey's end,
Never again to fall into the jaws of death.
With a discriminating intellect
As charioteer, a well-trained mind as reins,
They attain the supreme goal of life,
To be united with the Lord of Love.

The senses derive from objects of sense-perception,
Sense-objects from mind, mind from intellect,
And intellect from ego; ego from undifferentiated
Consciousness, and consciousness from Brahman.
Brahman is the first Cause and last refuge.
Brahman, the hidden Self in everyone,
Does not shine forth. He is revealed only
To those who keep their minds one-pointed
On the Lord of Love and thus develop
A superconscious manner of knowing.
Meditation empowers them to go
Deeper and deeper into consciousness,
From the world of words to the world of thought,
Then beyond thoughts to wisdom in the Self.

Get up! Wake up! Seek the guidance of an
Illumined teacher and realize the Self.
Sharp like a razor's edge is the path,
The sages say, difficult to traverse.

The supreme Self is beyond name and form,
Beyond the senses, inexhaustible,
Without beginning, without end,
Beyond time, space, and causality, eternal,
Immutable. Those who realize the Self
Are forever free from the jaws of death.

The wise, who gain experiential knowledge
Of this timeless tale of Nachiketa
Narrated by Death, attain the glory
Of living in spiritual awareness.
Those who, full of devotion, recite this
Supreme mystery at a spiritual
Gathering are fit for eternal life.
They are indeed fit for eternal life.

Sabbath Prayer

Only for God doth my soul wait in stillness;
    from Him cometh my hope.
He alone is my rock and my salvation, I shall not be moved.
Show me Thy ways, O Lord; teach me Thy paths,
    guide me in Thy truth.
Whom have I in heaven but Thee? And having Thee
    I desire none else upon earth.
My flesh and my heart fail, but God is my strength
    and my portion forever.
Wait for the Lord, be strong, and let thy heart take courage.
Create in me a clean heart, O God;
    and renew a steadfast spirit within me.
When many cares perplex me, Thy comfort delights my soul.
My times are in Thy hand, and Thou wilt guide and
    sustain me even unto the end.
With Thee is the fountain of life; in Thy light do we see light.

The Nectar of Immortality

The mind may be said to be of two kinds,
Pure and impure. Driven by the senses
It becomes impure; but with the senses
Under control, the mind becomes pure.

It is the mind that frees us or enslaves.
Driven by the senses we become bound;
Master of the senses we become free.
Those who seek freedom must master their senses.

When the mind is detached from the senses
One reaches the summit of consciousness.
Mastery of the mind leads to wisdom.
Practice meditation. Stop all vain talk.
The highest state is beyond reach of thought,
For it lies beyond all duality.

Keep repeating the ancient mantram O M
Until it reverberates in your heart.

Brahman is indivisible and pure;
Realize Brahman and go beyond all change.
He is immanent and transcendent.
Realizing him, sages attain freedom
And declare there are no separate minds.
They have but realized what they always are.

Waking, sleeping, dreaming, the Self is one.
Transcend these three and go beyond rebirth.
There is only one Self in all creatures.
The One appears many, just as the moon
Appears many, reflected in water.

The Self appears to change its location
But does not, just as air in a jar
Changes not when the jar is moved about.
When the jar is broken, the air knows not;
But the Self knows well when the body is shed.

We see not the Self, concealed by maya;
When the veil falls, we see we are the Self.

The mantram is the symbol of Brahman;
Repeating it can bring peace to the mind.

Knowledge is twofold, lower and higher.
Realize the Self; for all else is lower.
Realization is rice; all else is chaff.

The milk of cows of any hue is white.
The sages say that wisdom is the milk
And the sacred scriptures are the cows.

As butter lies hidden within milk,
The Self is hidden in the hearts of all.
Churn the mind through meditation on it;
Light your fire through meditation on it:
The Self, all whole, all peace, all certitude.

"I have realized the Self," declares the sage,
"Who is present in all beings.
I am united with the Lord of Love;
I am united with the Lord of Love."

The Nectar of Immortality

Twin Verses

All that we are is the result of what we have thought: we are formed and molded by our thoughts. Those whose minds are shaped by selfish thoughts cause misery when they speak or act. Sorrows roll over them as the wheels of a cart roll over the tracks of the bullock that draws it.

All that we are is the result of what we have thought: we are formed and molded by our thoughts. Those whose minds are shaped by selfless thoughts give joy whenever they speak or act. Joy follows them like a shadow that never leaves them.

"He insulted me, he struck me, he cheated me, he robbed me": those caught in resentful thoughts never find peace.

"He insulted me, he struck me, he cheated me, he robbed me": those who give up resentful thoughts surely find peace.

For hatred does not cease by hatred at any time: hatred ceases by love. This is an unalterable law.

There are those who forget that death will come to all. For those who remember, quarrels come to an end.

Those who live only for pleasure, who eat intemperately, who are lazy and weak and lack control over their senses, are like a tree with shallow roots. As a strong wind uproots such a tree, Mara the Tempter will throw such a person down.

But those who live without looking for pleasure, who eat temperately and control their senses, who are persevering and firm in faith, are like a mountain. As a strong wind cannot uproot a mountain, Mara cannot throw such a person down.

Whoever puts on the saffron robe but is self-willed, speaks untruthfully, and lacks self-control is not worthy of that sacred garment.

But those who have vanquished self-will, who speak the truth and have mastered themselves, are firmly established on the spiritual path and worthy of the saffron robe.

The deluded, imagining trivial things to be vital to life, follow their vain fancies and never attain the highest knowledge.

But the wise, knowing what is trivial and what is vital, set their thoughts on the supreme goal and attain the highest knowledge.

As rain seeps through a poorly thatched roof, passion seeps into the untrained mind.

As rain cannot seep through a well-thatched roof, passion cannot seep into a well-trained mind.

Those who are selfish suffer here and suffer there; they suffer wherever they go. They suffer and fret over the damage they have done.

But those who are selfless rejoice here and rejoice there; they rejoice wherever they go. They rejoice and delight in the good they have done.

The selfish person suffers here, and he suffers there; he suffers wherever he goes. He suffers as he broods over the damage he has done. He suffers more and more as he travels along the path of sorrow.

The selfless person is happy here, and he is happy there; he is happy wherever he goes. He is happy when he thinks of the good he has done. He grows in happiness as he progresses along the path of bliss.

Those who recite many scriptures but do not practice their teachings are like a cowherd counting another's cows. They do not share in the joys of the spiritual life.

But those who may know few scriptures but practice their teachings, who overcome all lust, hatred, and delusion, live with a pure mind in the highest wisdom. They stand without external supports and share in the joys of the spiritual life.

The Earth Is the Lord's

The earth is the Lord's, and the fullness thereof;
　　the world, and they that dwell therein.
For He hath founded it upon the seas,
　　and established it upon the floods.
Who shall ascend into the mountain of the Lord?
　　And who shall stand in His holy place?
He that hath clean hands, and a pure heart;
　　who hath not taken His name in vain,
　　and hath not sworn deceitfully.
He shall receive a blessing from the Lord,
　　and righteousness from the God of his salvation.
Such is the generation of them that seek after Him,
　　that seek Thy face, even Jacob.
Lift up your heads, O ye gates,
　　and be ye lifted up, ye everlasting doors;
　　that the King of glory may come in.
Who is the King of glory? The Lord strong and mighty,
　　the Lord mighty in battle.
Lift up your heads, O ye gates,
　　yea, lift them up,
　　ye everlasting doors;
　　that the King of glory may come in.
Who then is the King of glory?
　　The Lord of hosts; He is the King of glory.

The Lord of Life

May we harness body and mind to see
The Lord of Life who dwells in everyone.
May we with a one-pointed mind
Ever strive for blissful union with the Lord.
May we train our senses to serve the Lord
Through the practice of meditation.

Great is the glory of the Lord of Life,
Infinite, omnipresent, all-knowing.
He is known by the wise who meditate
And conserve their vital energy.

Hear, O children of immortal bliss!
You are born to be united with the Lord.
Follow the path of the illumined ones,
And be united with the Lord of Life.

Ignite kundalini in the depths of
Meditation. Bring your breathing and mind
Under control. Drink deep of divine love,
And you will attain the unitive state.

Dedicate yourself to the Lord of Life,
Who is the cause of the cosmos. He will
Remove the cause of all your suffering
And free you from the bondage of karma.

Be seated with spinal column erect
And turn your mind and senses deep within.
With the mantram echoing in your heart,
Cross over the dread sea of birth and death.

Train your senses to be obedient.
Regulate your activities to lead you
To the goal. Hold the reins of your mind
As you hold the reins of restive horses.

Choose a place for meditation that is
Clean, quiet, and cool, a cave with a smooth floor
Without stones and dust, protected against
Wind and rain and pleasing to the eye.

In deep meditation aspirants may
See forms like snow or smoke. They may feel
A strong wind blowing or a wave of heat.
They may see within them more and more light,
Fireflies, lightning, sun, or moon. These are signs
That they are well on their way to Brahman.

Health, a light body, freedom from cravings,
Clear skin, sonorous voice, fragrance
Of body: these signs indicate progress
In the practice of meditation.

As a dusty mirror shines bright when cleansed,
So shines the one who realizes the Self,
Attains life's goal, and passes beyond sorrow.

In the supreme climax of samadhi
He realizes the presence of the Lord
In his heart. Freed from all impurities,
He goes beyond birth and death.

The Lord dwells in the womb of the cosmos,
The Creator who is in all creatures.
He is that which is born and to be born;
His face is everywhere.

Let us adore the Lord of Life, who is
Present in fire and water, plants and trees.
Let us adore the Lord of Life!
Let us adore the Lord of Life!

The Mirror of Eternity

Place your mind before the mirror of eternity,
place your soul in the brightness of His glory,
place your heart in the image of the divine essence
and transform yourself by contemplation
    utterly into the image of His divinity,
that you too may feel what His friends feel as they taste
    the hidden sweetness that God himself has set aside
    from the beginning for those who love Him.

Casting aside all things in this false and troubled world
    that ensnare those who love them blindly,
    give all your love to Him who gave Himself in all
    for you to love:
Whose beauty the sun and moon admire, and whose gifts
    are abundant and precious and grand without end.

Such Is a Saint!

When the heart burns at the sufferings of others,
That is God's own heart.

When eyes strain to see others happy,
Through them God Himself sees.

When hands toil for others' relief,
These hands move only by God's will.

When the tongue sings His Name,
That voice is the voice of God.

Such is a Saint – God's own image!

The Central Truth

Forget not the central truth that God is seated
    in your own heart.
Don't be disheartened by failures at initial stages.
Cultivate the spirit of surrender to the workings of his will,
    inside you and outside you, until you have
    completely surrendered up your ego-sense
    and have known that he is in all, and he is all,
    and you and he are one.
Be patient. The path of self-discipline that leads to
    God-realization is not an easy path: obstacles
    and sufferings are on the path; the latter you must bear,
    and the former overcome – all by his help.
His help comes only through concentration.
Repetition of God's name helps concentration.

Prayer for the Peace of the World

O Thou, the Almighty Sun,
    whose light cleareth away all clouds,
    we take refuge in Thee,
    King of men, God of all deities,
    Lord of all angels.
We pray Thee
    dispel the mists of illusion
    from the hearts of the nations
    and lift their lives
    by Thy all-sufficient power.
Pour upon them
    Thy limitless love
    Thy everlasting life
    Thy heavenly joy
    and Thy perfect peace.

Khatum

O Thou,
>Who art the Perfection of
>Love, Harmony, and Beauty,
>The Lord of heaven and earth,

Open our hearts,
>That we may hear Thy Voice,
>Which constantly cometh from within.

Disclose to us Thy Divine Light,
>which is hidden in our souls,
>that we may know and understand life better.

Most Merciful and Compassionate God,
>Give us Thy great Goodness;
>Teach us Thy loving Forgiveness;
>Raise us above the distinctions and
>differences which divide us;

Send us the Peace of Thy Divine Spirit,
And unite us all in Thy Perfect Being.

The river of love overflows its banks,

and the lotus blooms in the devotee's heart.

—KABIR

PART 2

Deep Currents

Invocations

1

May the Lord of Love protect us.
May the Lord of Love nourish us.
May the Lord of Love strengthen us.
May we realize the Lord of Love.
May we live with love for all;
May we live in peace with all.

2

May the Lord of day grant us peace.
May the Lord of night grant us peace.
May the Lord of sight grant us peace.
May the Lord of might grant us peace.
May the Lord of speech grant us peace.
May the Lord of space grant us peace.
I bow down to Brahman, source of all power.
I will speak the truth and follow the law.
Guard me and my teacher against all harm.
Guard me and my teacher against all harm.

United in Heart

May we be united in heart.
May we be united in speech.
May we be united in mind.
May we perform our duties
As did the wise of old.

May we be united in our prayer.
May we be united in our goal.
May we be united in our resolve.
May we be united in our understanding.
May we be united in our offering.
May we be united in our feelings.
May we be united in our hearts.
May we be united in our thoughts.
May there be perfect unity amongst us.

The Shema

Hear, O Israel,
the Lord our God, the Lord is one.
Blessed is his name,
whose glorious kingdom is forever.

And you shall love the Lord with all your heart,
and with all your soul, and with all your might.

And these words, which I command you this
day, shall be upon your heart: and you shall
teach them always to your children, and shall
talk of them when you sit in your house, when
you walk by the way, when you lie down, and
when you arise.

And you shall bind them as a sign on your
hand, and they will be seen as a badge between
your eyes.

And you shall write them on the doorposts of
your house, and upon your gates.

Discourse on Good Will

May all beings be filled with joy and peace.
May all beings everywhere,
The strong and the weak,
The great and the small,
The mean and the powerful,
The short and the long,
The subtle and the gross:

May all beings everywhere,
Seen and unseen,
Dwelling far off or nearby,
Being or waiting to become:
May all be filled with lasting joy.

Let no one deceive another,
Let no one anywhere despise another,
Let no one out of anger or resentment
Wish suffering on anyone at all.

Just as a mother with her own life
Protects her child, her only child, from harm,
So within yourself let grow
A boundless love for all creatures.

Let your love flow outward through the universe,
To its height, its depth, its broad extent,
A limitless love, without hatred or enmity.

Then, as you stand or walk,
Sit or lie down,
As long as you are awake,
Strive for this with a one-pointed mind;
Your life will bring heaven to earth.

The Sermon on the Mount

1

Blessed are the poor in spirit:
    for theirs is the kingdom of heaven.

Blessed are they that mourn:
    for they shall be comforted.

Blessed are the meek:
    for they shall inherit the earth.

Blessed are they which do hunger and thirst
    after righteousness:
    for they shall be filled.

Blessed are the merciful:
    for they shall obtain mercy.

Blessed are the pure in heart:
    for they shall see God.

Blessed are the peacemakers:
    for they shall be called the children of God.

Blessed are they which are persecuted
    for righteousness' sake:
    for theirs is the kingdom of heaven.

Blessed are ye, when men shall revile you, and persecute you, and shall say all manner of evil against you falsely, for my sake. Rejoice, and be exceeding glad: for great is your reward in heaven: for so persecuted they the prophets which were before you.

Ye are the salt of the earth: but if the salt have lost his savor, wherewith shall it be salted? It is thenceforth good for nothing, but to be cast out, and to be trodden under foot of men.

Ye are the light of the world. A city that is set on a hill cannot be hid. Neither do men light a candle, and put it under a bushel, but on a candlestick; and it giveth light unto all that are in the house. Let your light so shine before men, that they may see your good works, and glorify your Father which is in heaven.

2

Ye have heard that it hath been said,
Thou shalt love thy neighbor, and hate thine enemy.
But I say unto you,

Love your enemies, bless them that curse you, do good to them that hate you, and pray for them which despitefully use you, and persecute you; that ye may be the children of your Father which is in heaven: for he maketh his sun to rise on the evil and on the good, and sendeth rain on the just and on the unjust.

For if ye love them which love you, what reward have ye? Do not even the publicans the same? And if ye salute your brethren only, what do ye more than others? Do not even the publicans so?

Be ye therefore perfect,
even as your Father which is in heaven is perfect.

3

Our Father which art in heaven, hallowed be thy name.
Thy kingdom come,
Thy will be done in earth, as it is in heaven.
Give us this day our daily bread,
And forgive us our debts, as we forgive our debtors.
And lead us not into temptation, but deliver us from evil:
For thine is the kingdom, and the power, and the glory,
    for ever.

SAINT FRANCIS OF ASSISI
The Prayer of Saint Francis

Lord, make me an instrument of thy peace.
Where there is hatred, let me sow love;
Where there is injury, pardon;
Where there is doubt, faith;
Where there is despair, hope;
Where there is darkness, light;
Where there is sadness, joy.

O divine Master, grant that I may not so much seek
To be consoled as to console,
To be understood as to understand,
To be loved as to love;
For it is in giving that we receive;
It is in pardoning that we are pardoned;
It is in dying to self that we are born to eternal life.

The Way of Love

ARJUNA:

Of those who love you as the Lord of Love,
Ever present in all, and those who seek you
As the nameless, formless Reality,
Which way is sure and swift, love or knowledge?

SRI KRISHNA:

For those who set their hearts on me
And worship me with unfailing devotion and faith,
The way of love leads sure and swift to me.

Those who seek the transcendental Reality,
Unmanifested, without name or form,
Beyond the reach of feeling and of thought,
With their senses subdued and mind serene
And striving for the good of all beings,
They too will verily come unto me.

Yet hazardous
And slow is the path to the Unrevealed,
Difficult for physical man to tread.
But they for whom I am the goal supreme,
Who do all work renouncing self for me
And meditate on me with single-hearted
Devotion, these will I swiftly rescue
From the fragment's cycle of birth and death
To fullness of eternal life in me.

Still your mind in me, still yourself in me,
And without doubt you shall be united with me,
Lord of Love, dwelling in your heart.
But if you cannot still your mind in me,
Learn to do so through the practice of meditation.
If you lack the will for such self-discipline,
Engage yourself in selfless service of all around you,
For selfless service can lead you at last to me.
If you are unable to do even this,
Surrender yourself to me in love,
Receiving success and failure with equal calmness
As granted by me.

Better indeed is knowledge than mechanical practice.
Better than knowledge is meditation.
But better still is surrender in love,
Because there follows immediate peace.

That one I love who is incapable of ill will,
And returns love for hatred.
Living beyond the reach of *I* and *mine*
And of pleasure and pain, full of mercy,
Contented, self-controlled, firm in faith,
With all their heart and all their mind given to me –
With such as these I am in love.

Not agitating the world or by it agitated,
They stand above the sway of elation,
Competition, and fear, accepting life
Good and bad as it comes. They are pure,
Efficient, detached, ready to meet every demand
I make on them as a humble instrument of my work.

They are dear to me who run not after the pleasant
Or away from the painful, grieve not
Over the past, lust not today,
But let things come and go as they happen.

Who serve both friend and foe with equal love,
Not buoyed up by praise or cast down by blame,
Alike in heat and cold, pleasure and pain,
Free from selfish attachments and self-will,
Ever full, in harmony everywhere,
Firm in faith – such as these are dear to me.

But dearest to me are those who seek me
In faith and love as life's eternal goal.
They go beyond death to immortality.

Dive Deep, O Mind

Dive deep, O mind, dive deep in the Ocean of God's Beauty;
If you descend to the uttermost depths,
There you will find the gem of Love.

Go seek, O mind, go seek Vrindavan in your heart,
Where with His loving devotees
Sri Krishna sports eternally.

Light up, O mind, light up true wisdom's shining lamp,
And let it burn with steady flame
Unceasingly within your heart.

Who is it that steers your boat across the solid earth?
It is your guru, says Kubir;
Meditate on his holy feet.

I Have Joined My Heart to Thee

I have joined my heart to Thee: all that exists art Thou;
Thee only have I found, for Thou art all that exists.
O Lord, Beloved of my heart! Thou art the Home of all;
Where indeed is the heart in which Thou dost not dwell?

Thou hast entered every heart: all that exists art Thou.
Whether sage or fool, whether Hindu or Mussalmān,
Thou makest them as Thou wilt: all that exists art Thou.

Thy presence is everywhere, whether in heaven or in Kaabā;
Before Thee all must bow, for Thou art all that exists.

From earth below to the highest heaven, from heaven
    to deepest earth,
I see Thee wherever I look: all that exists art Thou.

Pondering, I have understood; I have seen it beyond a doubt;
I find not a single thing that may be compared to Thee.
To Jāfar it has been revealed that Thou art all that exists.

O My God, Trinity Whom I Adore

O my God,
Trinity whom I adore,
help me to forget myself entirely
that I may be established in You
as still and as peaceful
as if my soul were already in eternity.
May nothing trouble my peace
or make me leave You,
O my Unchanging One,
but may each minute
carry me further
into the depths of Your Mystery.
Give peace to my soul;
make it Your heaven,
Your beloved dwelling
and Your resting place.
May I never leave You there alone
but be wholly present,
my faith wholly vigilant,
wholly adoring,
and wholly surrendered
to Your creative Action.

The Path to Your Dwelling

How am I to come to you
When I stand outside a locked gate?
The path to your dwelling
Runs steep and dangerous.
In fear I climb, step by step,
The path to your dwelling,
So steep and dangerous.
O Lord, you seem so far away
That my mind goes up and down.
As I climb, the sentinels watch
And the robbers wait to waylay me.
Though the path to your dwelling
Is steep and dangerous,
You have called me home.
Meera's wanderings are ended.
She has found her way to your feet.

Come, Beloved

As the lotus dies without water,
As the night is blind without the moon,
So is my heart without you, Beloved.
I wander alone at night,
Driven by my longing for you.
I hunger for you all the day,
I thirst for you all the night.

My grief is beyond words;
My mind is beyond rest.
Come and end my grief, Beloved.
Come and bring joy to my heart.
You know my inmost secret;
Then look at me with eyes of love,
Your slave for countless lives
    since the dawn of time.
So says Meera at your feet.

Life of My Life

You are the life of my life,
O Krishna, the heart of my heart.
There is none in all the three worlds
Whom I call my own but you.

You are the peace of my mind;
You are the joy of my heart;
You are my beauty and my wealth.

You are my wisdom and my strength;
I call you my home, my friend, my kin.

My present and future are in your hands;
My scriptures and commands come from you.
Supreme teacher, fountain of wisdom,
You are the path and the goal,
Tender mother and stern father too.

You are the creator and protector,
And the pilot who takes me across
The stormy ocean of life.

Lord, I Bring Thee My Treasure

Lord, I bring Thee my treasure!
It is greater than the mountains,
Wider than the world,
Deeper than the sea,
Higher than the clouds,
More glorious than the sun,
More manifold than the stars;
It outweighs the whole earth.

O thou image of My Divine Godhead,
Ennobled by My humanity,
Adorned by My Holy Spirit,
What is thy treasure called?

Lord, it is called my heart's desire.
I have withdrawn it from the world
And denied it to myself and all creatures.
Now I can bear it no longer.
Where, O Lord, shall I lay it?

Thy heart's desire shalt thou lay nowhere
But in Mine own Divine Heart
And on My human breast.
There alone wilt thou find comfort
And be embraced by My Holy Spirit.

Night Prayer

My God and my Lord,
    eyes are at rest,
    stars are setting,
    hushed are the movements of birds
      in their nests,
    of monsters in the deep.
And Thou art the Just who knowest no change,
    the Equity that swerveth not,
    the Everlasting that passeth not away.

The doors of kings are locked,
    watched by their bodyguards;
    but Thy door is open to him who calls on Thee.
My Lord, each lover is now alone with his beloved,
    and Thou art for me the Beloved.

Dawn Prayer

O God, the night has passed and the day has dawned.
How I long to know if Thou hast accepted my prayers
    or if Thou hast rejected them. Therefore console me,
    for it is Thine to console this state of mine.
Thou hast given me life and cared for me
    and Thine is the glory. If Thou wert to drive me from
    Thy door, yet would I not forsake it, for the love
    that I bear in my heart for Thee.

O my Joy and my Desire and my Refuge,
    my Friend and my Sustainer and my Goal,
    Thou art my Intimate, and longing for Thee sustains me.
Were it not for Thee, O my Life and my Friend,
    how I should have been distraught
    over the spaces of the earth!
How many favors have been bestowed,
    and how much hast Thou given me
    Of gifts and grace and assistance.
Thy love is now my desire and my bliss,
    and has been revealed to the eye of my heart
        that was athirst.
I have none beside Thee, Who dost make the desert blossom.
Thou art my joy, firmly established within me.
If Thou art satisfied with me, then,
    O Desire of my heart, my happiness has appeared!

I Am Thine, Lord

I am thine, Lord, and am to belong to none but to thee.
My soul is thine, and ought not to live but by thee;
   my will is thine, and ought not to love but for thee;
   my love is thine, and is only to tend to thee.
I am to love thee as my First Cause,
   since I have my being from thee.
I am to love thee as my end and center,
   since I am for thee.
I am to love thee more than my own being,
   since even my being does subsist by thee.
I am to love thee more than myself,
   since I am wholly thine and in thee.

RABBI ELEAZAR AZIKRI

Beloved of the Soul

Beloved of the soul, source of compassion,
Shape your servant to your will.
Then your servant will run like a deer to bow before you.
Your love will be sweeter than a honeycomb.
Majestic, beautiful, light of the universe,
My soul is lovesick for you;
I implore you, God, heal her
By revealing to her your pleasant radiance;
Then she will be strengthened and healed
And will have eternal joy.
Timeless One, be compassionate
And have mercy on the one you love,
For this is my deepest desire:
To see your magnificent splendor.
This is what my heart longs for;
Have mercy and do not conceal yourself.
Reveal yourself, my Beloved,
And spread the shelter of your peace over me;
Light up the world with your glory;
We will celebrate you in joy.
Hurry, Beloved, the time has come,
And grant us grace, as in days of old.

❧

The Wonderful Effect of Divine Love

1

Ah, Lord God, thou holy lover of my soul, when thou comest into my heart, all that is within me shall rejoice. Thou art my glory and the exultation of my heart: thou art my hope and refuge in the day of my trouble.

2

But because I am as yet weak in love, and imperfect in virtue, I have need to be strengthened and comforted by thee; visit me therefore often, and instruct me with all holy discipline.

Set me free from evil passions, and heal my heart of all inordinate affections; that being inwardly cured and thoroughly cleansed, I may be made fit to love, courageous to suffer, steady to persevere.

3

Love is a great thing, yea, a great and thorough good; by itself it makes every thing that is heavy, light; and it bears evenly all that is uneven. For it carries a burden which is no burden, and makes every thing that is bitter, sweet and tasteful.

The noble love of Jesus impels one to do great things, and stirs one up to be always longing for what is more perfect.

Love desires to be aloft, and will not be kept back by any thing low and mean.

Love desires to be free, and estranged from all worldly affections, that so its inward sight may not be hindered; that it may not be entangled by any temporal prosperity, or by any adversity subdued.

Nothing is sweeter than love, nothing more courageous, nothing higher, nothing wider, nothing more pleasant, nothing fuller nor better in heaven and earth; because love is born of God, and cannot rest but in God, above all created things.

4

He that loveth, flyeth, runneth, and rejoiceth; he is free, and cannot be held in.

He giveth all for all, and hath all in all; because he resteth in One highest above all things, from whom all that is good flows and proceeds.

He respecteth not the gifts, but turneth himself above all goods unto the Giver.

Love often times knoweth no measure, but is fervent beyond all measure.

Love feels no burden, thinks nothing of trouble, attempts what is above its strength, pleads no excuse of impossibility; for it thinks all things lawful for itself and all things possible.

It is therefore able to undertake all things, and it completes many things, and warrants them to take effect, where he who does not love would faint and lie down.

5

Love is watchful, and sleeping slumbereth not.

Though weary, it is not tired; though pressed, it is not straitened; though alarmed, it is not confounded; but as a lively flame and burning torch, it forces its way upwards, and securely passes through all.

If any one love, he knoweth what is the cry of this voice. For it is a loud cry in the ears of God, the mere ardent affection of the soul, when it saith, "My God, my love, thou art all mine, and I am all thine."

6

Enlarge thou me in love, that with the inward palate of my heart I may taste how sweet it is to love, and to be dissolved, and as it were to bathe myself in thy love.

Let me be possessed by love, mounting above myself, through excessive fervor and admiration.

Let me sing the song of love, let me follow thee, my Beloved, on high; let my soul spend itself in thy praise, rejoicing through love.

Let me love thee more than myself, nor love myself but for thee: and in thee all that truly love thee, as the law of love commandeth, shining out from thyself.

7

Love is active, sincere, affectionate, pleasant and amiable; courageous, patient, faithful, prudent, long-suffering, resolute, and never seeking itself.

For in whatever instance one seeketh oneself, there he falleth from love.

Love is circumspect, humble, and upright: not yielding to softness, or to levity, nor attending to vain things; it is sober, chaste, steady, quiet, and guarded in all the senses.

Love is subject, and obedient to its superiors, to itself mean and despised, unto God devout and thankful, trusting and hoping always in Him, even then when God imparteth no relish of sweetness unto it: for without sorrow, none liveth in love.

8

He that is not prepared to suffer all things, and to stand to the will of his Beloved, is not worthy to be called a lover of God.

A lover ought to embrace willingly all that is hard and distasteful, for the sake of his Beloved; and not to turn away from him for any contrary accidents.

Evening Prayer for the Sabbath

In this moment of silent communion with Thee,
    O Lord, a still small voice speaks in the depth
    of my spirit.
It speaks to me of the things I must do to attain
    holy kinship with Thee and to grow
    in the likeness of Thee.
I must do my allotted task with unflagging faithfulness
    even though the eye of no taskmaster is on me.
I must be gentle in the face of ingratitude
    or when slander distorts my noblest motives.
I must come to the end of each day with a feeling
    that I have used its gifts gratefully
    and faced its trials bravely.
O Lord, help me to be ever more like Thee,
    holy for Thou art holy,
    loving for Thou art love.
Speak to me, then, Lord, as I seek Thee again and again
    in the stillness of meditation, until Thy bidding
    shall at last become for me a hallowed discipline,
    a familiar way of life.

Just Because You Are My God

Oh, my God, I want to love you
Not that I might gain eternal heaven
Nor escape eternal hell
But, Lord, to love you just because
    you are my God.

Grant me to give to you
And not to count the cost,
To fight for you
And not to mind the wounds,
To labor and to ask for no reward
    except the knowledge
    that I serve my God.

Shine through Us

Dear Jesus, help us to spread your fragrance
  everywhere we go.
Flood our souls with your spirit and life.
Penetrate and possess our whole being so utterly
  that our lives may only be a radiance of yours.
Shine through us, and be so in us,
  that every soul we come in contact with
  may feel your presence in our soul.
Let them look up and see no longer us
  but only Jesus!
Stay with us, and then we shall begin to shine
  as you shine; so to shine as to be a light to others;
  the light, O Jesus, will be all from you,
  none of it will be ours;
  it will be you, shining on others through us.
Let us thus praise you in the way you love best
  by shining on those around us.
Let us preach you without preaching, not by words
  but by our example, by the catching force,
  the sympathetic influence of what we do,
  the evident fullness of the love
  our hearts bear to you.

Invocations

In the name of God,
Most gracious,
Most merciful.

O thou munificent one
Who art the bestower of all bounties,
O thou wise one
Who overlookest our faults,
O self-existent one
Who art beyond our comprehension,
O thou omnipotent one
Who hast no equal in power and greatness,
Who art without a second:
O thou merciful one
Who guidest stray souls to the right path,
Thou art truly our God.

Give purity to our minds,
Aspiration to our hearts,
Light to our eyes.
Out of thy grace and bounty
Give us that which thou deemest best.

O Lord, out of thy grace
Give faith and light to our hearts,
And with the medicine of truth and steadfastness
Cure the ills of this life.

I know not what to ask of thee.
Thou art the knower;
Give what thou deemest best.

O God, may my brain reel with thoughts of thee,
May my heart thrill with the mysteries of thy grace,
May my tongue move only to utter thy praise.

I live only to do thy will;
My lips move only in praise of thee.
O Lord, whoever becometh aware of thee,
Casteth out all else other than thee.

O Lord, give me a heart
That I may pour it out in thanksgiving.
Give me life
That I may spend it in working
For the salvation of the world.

O Lord, give me that right discrimination
That the lure of the world may cheat me no more.
Give me strength
That my faith suffer no eclipse.

O Lord, give me understanding
That I stray not from the path.
Give me light
To avoid pitfalls.

O Lord, keep watch over me
That I stray not.
Keep me on the path of righteousness
That I escape from the pangs of repentance.

O Lord, judge me not by my actions.
Of thy mercy, save me,
And make my humble efforts fruitful.

O Lord, give me a heart
Free from the flames of desire.
Give me a mind
Free from the waves of egoism.

O Lord, give me eyes
Which see nothing but thy glory.
Give me a mind
That finds delight in thy service.
Give me a soul
Drunk in the wine of thy wisdom.

O Lord, to find thee is my desire,
But to comprehend thee is beyond my strength.
Remembering thee is solace to my sorrowing heart;
Thoughts of thee are my constant companions.
I call upon thee night and day.
The flame of thy love glows
In the darkness of my night.

Life in my body pulsates only for thee,
My heart beats in resignation to thy will.
If on my dust a tuft of grass were to grow,
Every blade would tremble with my devotion for thee.

O Lord, everyone desires to behold thee.
I desire that thou mayest cast a glance at me.
Let me not disgrace myself.
If thy forgiveness awaits me in the end,
Lower not the standard of forgiveness
Which thou hast unfurled.

O Lord, prayer at thy gate
Is a mere formality:
Thou knowest what thy slave desires.
O Lord, better for me to be dust

And my name effaced
From the records of the world
Than that thou forget me.

He knoweth all our good and evil.
Nothing is hidden from him.
He knoweth what is the best medicine
To cure the pain and to rescue the fallen.
Be humble, for he exalteth the humble.

I am intoxicated with love for thee
And need no fermented wine.
I am thy bird, free from need of seed
And safe from the snare of the fowler.
In the kaaba and in the temple,
Thou art the object of my search,
Else I am freed
From both these places of worship.

Lord, when thou wert hidden from me
The fever of life possessed me.
When thou revealest thyself
This fever of life departeth.

O Lord, other men are afraid of thee
But I - I am afraid of myself.
From thee flows good alone,
From me flows evil.
Others fear what the morrow may bring;
I am afraid of what happened yesterday.

O Lord, if thou holdest me responsible for my sins
I shall cling to thee for thy grace.
I with my sin am an insignificant atom.
Thy grace is resplendent as the sun.

O Lord, out of regard for thy name,
The qualities which are thine,
Out of regard for thy greatness,
Listen to my cry,
For thou alone canst redeem me.

O Lord, intoxicate me with the wine of thy love.
Place the chains of thy slavery on my feet;
Make me empty of all but thy love,
And in it destroy me and bring me back to life.
The hunger thou has awakened
Culminates in fulfillment.

Make my body impervious to the fires of hell;
Vouchsafe to me a vision of thee in heaven.
The spark thou hast kindled, make it everlasting.

I think of no other,
And in thy love care for none else.
None has a place in my heart but thee.
My heart has become thy abode;
It has no place for another.

O Lord, thou cherishest the helpless,
And I am helpless.
Apply thy balm to my bleeding heart,
For thou art the physician.

O Lord, I, a beggar, ask of thee
More than what a thousand kings may ask of thee.
Each one has something he needs to ask of thee;
I have come to ask thee to give me thyself.

If words can establish a claim,
I claim a crown.
But if deeds are wanted,
I am as helpless as the ant.

Urged by desire, I wandered
In the streets of good and evil.
I gained nothing except feeding the fire of desire.
As long as in me remains the breath of life,
Help me, for thou alone canst hear my prayer.

Watch vigilantly the state of thine own mind.
Love of God begins in harmlessness.

Know that the prophet built an external kaaba
Of clay and water,
And an inner kaaba in life and heart.
The outer kaaba was built by Abraham, the holy;
The inner is sanctified by the glory of God himself.

On the path of God
Two places of worship mark the stages,
The material temple
And the temple of the heart.
Make your best endeavor
To worship at the temple of the heart.

In this path, be one
With a heart full of compassion.
Engage not in vain doing;
Make not thy home in the street of lust and desire.

If thou wouldst become a pilgrim on the path of love,
The first condition is that thou become
As humble as dust and ashes.

Know that when thou learnest to lose thy self
Thou wilt reach the Beloved.
There is no other secret to be revealed,
And more than this is not known to me.

Be humble and cultivate silence.
If thou hast received, rejoice,
And fill thyself with ecstasy.
And if not, continue the demand.

What is worship?
To realize reality.
What is the sacred law?
To do no evil.
What is reality?
Selflessness.

The heart inquired of the soul,
What is the beginning of this business?
What its end, and what its fruit?
The soul answered:
The beginning of it is the annihilation of self,
Its end faithfulness,
And its fruit immortality.

The heart asked, what is annihilation?
What is faithfulness?
What is immortality?
The soul answered:
Freedom from self is annihilation.
Faithfulness is fulfillment of love.
Immortality is the union of immortal with mortal.

In this path the eye must cease to see
And the ear to hear,
Save unto him and about him.
Be as dust on his path;
Even the kings of this earth
Make the dust of his feet
The balm of their eyes.

Prayer for Peace

Adorable presence,
Thou who art within and without,
   above and below and all around,
Thou who art interpenetrating
   every cell of my being,
Thou who art the eye of my eyes,
   the ear of my ears,
   the heart of my heart,
   the mind of my mind,
   the breath of my breath,
   the life of my life,
   the soul of my soul,
Bless us, dear God, to be aware of thy presence
   now and here.

May we all be aware of thy presence
   in the East and the West,
   in the North and the South.
May peace and goodwill abide among individuals,
   communities, and nations.
This is my earnest prayer.

May peace be unto all!

Prayer for Peace

Send us Thy peace, O Lord,
    which is perfect and everlasting,
    that our souls may radiate peace.
Send us Thy peace, O Lord,
    that we may think, act, and speak harmoniously.
Send us Thy peace, O Lord,
    that we may be contented and
    thankful for Thy bountiful gifts.
Send us Thy peace, O Lord,
    that amidst our worldly strife
    we may enjoy Thy bliss.
Send us Thy peace, O Lord,
    that we may endure all, tolerate all
    in the thought of Thy grace and mercy.
Send us Thy peace, O Lord,
    that our lives may become a divine vision,
    and in Thy light all darkness may vanish.
Send us Thy peace, O Lord,
    our Father and Mother,
    that we, Thy children on earth,
    may all unite in one family.

Epistle on Love

If I speak in the tongues of men and of angels, but have not love, I am a noisy gong or a clanging cymbal. And if I have prophetic powers, and understand all mysteries and all knowledge, and if I have all faith, so as to remove mountains, but have not love, I am nothing. If I give away all I have, and if I deliver my body to be burned, but have not love, I gain nothing.

Love is patient and kind; love is not jealous or boastful; it is not arrogant or rude. Love does not insist on its own way; it is not irritable or resentful; it does not rejoice at wrong, but rejoices in the right. Love bears all things, believes all things, hopes all things, endures all things.

Love never ends; as for prophecies, they will pass away; as for tongues, they will cease; as for knowledge, it will pass away. For our knowledge is imperfect and our prophecy is imperfect; but when the perfect comes, the imperfect will pass away.

When I was a child, I spoke like a child, I thought like a child, I reasoned like a child; when I became a man, I gave up childish ways. For now we see in a mirror dimly, but then face to face. Now I know in part; then I shall understand fully, even as I have been fully understood.

So faith, hope, love abide, these three; but the greatest of these is love.

The Best

The best, like water,
Benefit all and do not compete.
They dwell in lowly spots that everyone else scorns.
Putting others before themselves,
They find themselves in the foremost place
And come very near to the Tao.
In their dwelling, they love the earth;
In their heart, they love what is deep;
In personal relationships, they love kindness;
In their words, they love truth.
In the world, they love peace.
In personal affairs, they love what is right.
In action, they love choosing the right time.
It is because they do not compete with others
That they are beyond the reproach of the world.

Give Up Anger

Give up anger, give up pride, and free yourself from worldly bondage. No sorrow can befall those who never try to possess people and things as their own.

Those who hold back rising anger like a rolling chariot are real charioteers. Others merely hold the reins.

Conquer anger through gentleness, unkindness through kindness, greed through generosity, and falsehood by truth. Be truthful; do not yield to anger. Give freely, even if you have but little. The gods will bless you.

Injuring no one, self-controlled, the wise enter the state of peace beyond all sorrow. Those who are vigilant, who train their minds day and night and strive continually for nirvana, enter the state of peace beyond all selfish passions.

There is an old saying: "People will blame you if you say too much; they will blame you if you say too little; they will blame you if you say just enough." No one in this world escapes blame.

There never was and never will be anyone who receives all praise or all blame. But who can blame those who are pure, wise, good, and meditative? They shine like a coin of pure gold. Even the gods praise them, even Brahma the Creator.

Use your body for doing good, not for harm.
Train it to follow the dharma.

Use your tongue for doing good, not for harm.
Train it to speak kindly.

Use your mind for doing good, not for harm.
Train your mind in love.

The wise are disciplined in body, speech, and mind.
They are well controlled indeed.

The Way to Peace

If anyone speaks ill of you,
Praise him always.

If anyone injures you,
Serve him nicely.

If anyone persecutes you,
Help him in all possible ways.

You will attain immense strength.

You will control anger and pride.

You will enjoy peace, poise and serenity.

You will become divine.

LAO TZU

Finding Unity

Those who know do not speak;
Those who speak do not know.
Stop up the openings,
Close down the doors,
Rub off the sharp edges.
Unravel all confusion.
Harmonize the light,
Give up contention:
This is called finding the unity of life.

When love and hatred cannot affect you,
Profit and loss cannot touch you,
Praise and blame cannot ruffle you,
You are honored by all the world.

ISAIAH

When You Call

Then, when you call, the Lord will answer;
When you cry, He will say: Here I am.
If you banish the yoke from your midst,
The menacing hand and evil speech,
And you offer your compassion to the hungry
And satisfy the famished creature –
Then shall your light shine in darkness,
And your gloom shall be like noonday.
The Lord will guide you always;
He will slake your thirst in parched places
And give strength to your bones.
You shall be like a watered garden,
Like a spring whose waters do not fail.

The Whole World Is Your Own

I tell you one thing –
If you want peace of mind,
do not find fault with others.

Rather learn to see your own faults.
Learn to make the whole world your own.

No one is a stranger, my child;
this whole world is your own.

The Real Lovers of God

They are the real lovers of God
Who feel others' sorrow as their own.
When they perform selfless service,
They are humble servants of the Lord.
Respecting all, despising none,
They are pure in thought, word, and deed.
Blessed is the mother of such a child,
And in their eyes the Divine Mother
Shines in every woman they see.
They are always truthful, even-minded,
Never coveting others' wealth,
Free from all selfish attachments,
Ever in tune with the Holy Name.
Their bodies are like sacred shrines
In which the Lord of Love is seen.
Free from greed, anger, and fear,
These are the real lovers of God.

Christ Be with Me

May the strength of God pilot me,
the power of God preserve me today.
May the wisdom of God instruct me,
the eye of God watch over me,
the ear of God hear me,
the word of God give me sweet talk,
the hand of God defend me,
the way of God guide me.

Christ be with me.
Christ before me.
Christ after me.
Christ in me.
Christ under me.
Christ over me.
Christ on my right hand.
Christ on my left hand.
Christ on this side.
Christ on that side.
Christ at my back.

Christ in the head of everyone to whom I speak.
Christ in the mouth of every person who speaks to me.

Christ in the eye of every person who looks at me.
Christ in the ear of every person who hears me today.

Silence

I weave a silence onto my lips.
I weave a silence into my mind.
I weave a silence within my heart.
I close my ears to distractions.
I close my eyes to attractions.
I close my heart to temptations.

Calm me, O Lord, as you stilled the storm.
Still me, O Lord, keep me from harm.
Let all tumult within me cease.
Enfold me, Lord, in your peace.

This Morning I Pray

This morning, as I kindle the fire on my hearth,
  I pray that the flame of God's love may burn in
  my heart and in the hearts of all I meet today.

I pray that no envy or malice,
  no hatred or fear, may smother the flame.

I pray that indifference and apathy, contempt and pride,
  may not pour like cold water on the fire.

Instead, may the spark of God's love
  light the love in my heart,
  that it may burn brightly through the day.

And may I warm those who are lonely,
  whose hearts are cold and lifeless,
  so that all may know the comfort of God's love.

The Practice of the Presence of God

1

O my God, since thou art with me, and I must now, in obedience to thy commands, apply my mind to these outward things, I beseech thee to grant me the grace to continue in thy presence; and to this end do thou prosper me with thy assistance, receive all my works, and possess all my affections.

2

God knoweth best what is needful for us, and all that he does is for our good. If we knew how much he loves us, we should always be ready to receive equally and with indifference from his hand the sweet and the bitter. All would please that came from him. The sorest afflictions never appear intolerable, except when we see them in the wrong light. When we see them as dispensed by the hand of God, when we know that it is our loving Father who abases and distresses us, our sufferings will lose their bitterness and become even matter of consolation.

Let all our employment be to know God; the more one knows him, the more one desires to know him. And as knowledge is commonly the measure of love, the deeper and more extensive our knowledge shall be, the greater will be our love; and if our love of God were great, we should love him equally in pains and pleasures.

Let us not content ourselves with loving God for the mere sensible favors, how elevated soever, which he has done or may do us. Such favors, though never so great, cannot bring us so near to him as faith does in one simple act. Let us seek him often by faith. He is within us; seek him not elsewhere. If we do love him alone, are we not rude, and do we not deserve blame, if we busy ourselves about trifles which do not please and perhaps offend him? It is to be feared these trifles will one day cost us dear.

Let us begin to be devoted to him in good earnest.
Let us cast everything besides out of our hearts.
He would possess them alone. Beg this favor of him.
If we do what we can on our part, we shall soon see
that change wrought in us which we aspire after.

Duties of the Heart

What is meant by wholehearted devotion to God alone?

It means that in every act, public and private, the aim
and purpose should be purely work for God's sake,
to please him only, without winning the approval of
other people.

How achieve wholehearted devotion to God alone? In
ten ways. If these are firmly set in your heart and you
clearly make them the basis of your actions, then your
devotion to God will be complete. Then you will turn
to no one else, set your hope on nothing else, and mold
your will to none other than God's.

First is wholehearted acceptance that only God
fills the universe;

Second, that God is the source of all reality
and is endlessly good;

Third, that your goal is to work for God;

Fourth, that you should rely on God alone and not
physical beings;

Fifth, that you get no ultimate gain or loss
from physical beings, but only from the Creator;

Sixth, that you should maintain evenness of mind regardless of whether people praise you or blame you;

Seventh, that you should not make a show of spiritual activities to impress other people;

Eighth, that you should not be caught up in personal gain when you are working for eternal life;

Ninth, that you should hold God in reverence and be humble before him;

Tenth, that you should use your mind to master your senses and use them with care and discrimination.

You Are Christ's Hands

Christ has no body now on earth but yours,
    no hands but yours, no feet but yours,

Yours are the eyes through which is to look out
    Christ's compassion to the world;

Yours are the feet with which he is
    to go about doing good;

Yours are the hands with which he is
    to bless us now.

Unshakable Faith

Unshakable faith in God and His will:
Nothing short of this.
Take thorough refuge in Him.
Give up all fears,
    all anxieties, all doubts,
    all thoughts of weakness.
You have put yourself under the guidance and control
    of an all-powerful being.
Let Him do what He pleases with you.
Give up *I* and *mine*. Make no plans.
Let nothing of the past or future disturb you.
God is the sole doer and you are His child, His servant.
Your *I* and *mine* has no existence. It is all He, He alone.
Submit, resign, surrender yourself to Him.
Be always cheerful, peaceful, and blissful. In this state
    you will always remain. This is your goal.
God is always in you and you are always in Him.
He and you are one. This is the truth.

The Path of Love

O seeker of truth, it is your heart's eye you must open.
Know the Divine Unity today,
    through the path of love for Him.

If you object: "I am waiting for my mind to grasp His nature,"
Know the Divine Unity today,
    through the path of love for Him.

Should you wish to behold the face of God,
Surrender to Him, and invoke His names.

When your soul is clear, a light of true joy shall shine.
Know the Divine Unity today,
    through the path of love for Him.

Hidden in the Heart

Brahman, attributeless Reality,
Becomes the Lord of Love who casts his net
Of appearance over the cosmos and rules
It from within through his divine power.
He was before creation; he will be
After dissolution. He alone is.
Those who know him become immortal.

The Lord of Love is one. There is indeed
No other. He is the inner ruler
In all beings. He projects the cosmos
From himself, maintains and withdraws it
Back into himself at the end of time.

His eyes, mouths, arms, and feet are everywhere.
Projecting the cosmos out of himself,
He holds it together.
He is the source of all the powers of life.
He is the lord of all, the great seer
Who dwells forever in the cosmic womb.
May he purify our consciousness!
O Lord, in whom alone we can find peace,
May we see your divine Self and be freed
From all impure thoughts and all fear.

O Lord, from whom we receive the mantram
As a weapon to destroy our self-will,
Reveal yourself, protector of all.

You are the supreme Brahman, infinite,
Yet hidden in the hearts of all creatures.
You pervade everything. Realizing you,
We attain immortality.

I have realized the Lord of Love,
Who is the sun that dispels our darkness.
Those who realize him go beyond death;
No other way is there to immortality.

There is nothing higher than him, nothing other
Than him. His infinity is beyond great
And small. In his own glory rooted,
He stands and fills the cosmos.

He fills the cosmos, yet he transcends it.
Those who know him leave all separateness,
Sorrow, and death behind. Those who know him not
Live but to suffer.

The Lord of Love, omnipresent, dwelling
In the heart of every living creature,
All mercy, turns every face to himself.

He is the supreme Lord, who through his grace
Moves us to seek him in our own hearts.
He is the light that shines forever.

He is the inner Self of all,
Hidden like a little flame in the heart.
Only by the stilled mind can he be known.
Those who realize him become immortal.

He has thousands of heads, thousands of eyes,
Thousands of feet; he surrounds the cosmos
On every side. This infinite being
Is ever present in the hearts of all.

He has become the cosmos. He is what was
And what will be. Yet he is unchanging,
The lord of immortality.

His hands and feet are everywhere; his heads
And mouths everywhere. He sees everything,
Hears everything, and pervades everything.

Without organs of sense, he shines through them.
He is the lord of all, inner ruler,
Protector and friend of all.

He resides in the city with nine gates,
Which is the body. He moves in the world
Enjoying the play of his countless forms.
He is the master of the universe,
Of animate and inanimate.

He runs without feet and holds without hands.
He sees without eyes and hears without ears.
He knows everyone, but no one knows him.
He is called the First, the Great, the Supreme.

The Lord of Love is hidden in the heart
Of every creature, subtler than the subtlest,
Greater than the greatest. Through his grace
One sheds all selfish desires and sorrow
And becomes united with the Self.

I know this Self, sage Shvetashvatara said,
To be immortal and infinite.
I know this Self who is the Self of all,
Whom the sages call the Eternal One.

Living on Love

On the evening of love, speaking without parable,
Jesus said: "If anyone wishes to love me
All his life, let him keep my Word.
My Father and I will come to visit him.
And we will make his heart our dwelling.
Coming to him, we shall love him always.
We want him to remain, filled with peace,
    In our Love . . ."

Living on Love is holding You Yourself,
Uncreated Word, Word of my God.
Ah! Divine Jesus, you know I love you.
The Spirit of Love sets me aflame with his fire.
In loving you I attract the Father.
My weak heart holds him forever.
O Trinity! You are Prisoner
    Of my Love! . . .

Living on Love is living on your life,
Glorious King, delight of the elect.
You live for me, hidden in a host.
I want to hide myself in you, O Jesus!
Lovers must have solitude,
A heart-to-heart lasting night and day.
Just one glance of yours makes my beatitude.
    I live on Love! . . .

Living on Love is giving without limit
Without claiming any wages here below.
Ah! I give without counting, truly sure
That when one loves, one does not keep count! . . .
Overflowing with tenderness, I have given everything,
To his Divine Heart . . . lightly I run.
I have nothing left but my only wealth:
Living on Love.

Living on Love is banishing every fear,
Every memory of past faults.
I see no imprint of my sins.
In a moment love has burned everything . . .
Divine Flame, O very sweet Blaze!
I make my home in your hearth.
In your fire I gladly sing:
"I live on Love! . . ."

Living on Love is keeping within oneself
A great treasure in an earthen vase.
My Beloved, my weakness is extreme.
Ah, I'm far from being an angel from heaven!
But if I fall with each passing hour,
You come to my aid, lifting me up.
At each moment you give me your grace:
I live on Love.

Living on Love is sailing unceasingly,
Sowing peace and joy in every heart.
Beloved Pilot, Charity impels me,
For I see you in my sister souls.
Charity is my only star.
In its brightness I sail straight ahead.
I've my motto written on my sail:
"Living on Love."

Living on Love, when Jesus is sleeping,
Is rest on stormy seas.
Oh! Lord, don't fear that I'll wake you.
I'm waiting in peace for Heaven's shore . . .
Faith will soon tear its veil.
My hope is to see you one day.
Charity swells and pushes my sail:
       I live on Love! . . .

Dying of Love is what I hope for.
When I shall see my bonds broken,
My God will be my Great Reward.
I don't desire to possess other goods.
I want to be set on fire with his Love.
I want to see Him, to unite myself to Him forever.
That is my Heaven . . . that is my destiny:
       Living on Love!!! . . .

In Your Midst

I, God, am in your midst.

Whoever knows me can never fall,
Not in the heights,
Not in the depths,
Nor in the breadths,
For I am love,

Which the vast expanses of evil
Can never still.

Whatever You Do

A leaf, a flower, a fruit, or even
Water, offered to me in devotion,
I will accept as the loving gift
Of a dedicated heart. Whatever you do,
Make it an offering to me –
The food you eat or worship you perform,
The help you give, even your suffering.
Thus will you be free from karma's bondage,
From the results of action, good and bad.

I am the same to all beings. My love
Is the same always. Nevertheless, those
Who meditate on me with devotion,
They dwell in me, and I shine forth in them.

Even the worst sinner becomes a saint
When he loves me with all his heart. This love
Will soon transform his personality
And fill his heart with peace profound.
O son of Kunti, this is my promise:
Those who love me, they shall never perish.

Even those who are handicapped by birth
Have reached the supreme goal in life
By taking refuge in me. How much more
The pure brahmins and royal sages who love me!

Give not your love to this transient world
Of suffering, but give all your love to me.
Give me your mind, your heart, all your worship.
Long for me always, live for me always,
And you shall be united with me.

KABIR

The Unstruck Bells & Drums

The Lord is in me, the Lord is in you,
    as life is in every seed.
O servant! Put false pride away
    and seek for him within you.
A million suns are ablaze with light,
The sea of blue spreads in the sky,
The fever of life is stilled, and all stains
    are washed away
When I sit in the midst of that world.

Hark to the unstruck bells and drums!
Take your delight in love!
Rains pour down without water,
    and the rivers are streams of light.
One love it is that pervades the whole world;
    few there are who know it fully:
They are blind who hope to see it by the light of reason,
    that reason which is the cause of separation –
The house of reason is very far away!

How blessed is Kabir, that amidst this great joy
    he sings within his own vessel.
It is the music of the meeting of soul with soul;
It is the music of the forgetting of sorrows;
It is the music that transcends all coming in
    and all going forth.

The River of Love

I am a citizen of that kingdom
Where reigns the Lord in all His glory;
Neither pain nor pleasure cast their shadows
Where the sun of joy never sets.

I am a citizen of that kingdom
Where every day is a day of celebration;
The river of love overflows its banks,
And the lotus blooms in the devotee's heart.

I am a citizen of that kingdom
Where shines the Lord as the source of light,
And lights the lamp of wisdom in my heart
To burn without oil, without wick.

Simple Union

O seeker, the simple union is the best.
Since the day when I met with my Lord,
There has been no end to the sport of our love.
I shut not my eyes, I close not my ears,
I do not mortify my body; I see with eyes open
And smile and behold his beauty everywhere:
I utter his name, and whatever I see,
It reminds me of him; whatever I do,
It becomes his worship.
The rising and the setting are one to me:
All contradictions are solved.
Wherever I go, I move round him.
All I achieve is his service: when I lie down,
I lie prostrate at his feet.
He is the only adorable one to me:
I have none other.
My tongue has left off impure words;
It sings his glory, day and night.
Whether I rise or sit down, I can never forget him,
For the rhythm of his music beats in my ears.
Kabir says: My heart is frenzied
And I disclose in my soul what is hidden.
I am immersed in that great bliss
Which transcends all pleasure and pain.

He Is Omnipresent

In my heart I found my Beloved.
Now wherever I turn, His face I see
In all beings and things – great and small.
His light illumines all space.
He is there in nature's beauty.
He is present in men, birds, and beasts –
His power pervades all the worlds.
He is Love, Peace, and Joy.

I Gave All My Heart

I gave all my heart to the Lord of Love,
And my life is so completely transformed
That my Beloved One has become mine
And without a doubt I am his at last.

When that tender hunter from paradise
Released his piercing arrow at me,
My wounded soul fell in his loving arms;
And my life is so completely transformed
That my Beloved One has become mine
And without a doubt I am his at last.

He pierced my heart with his arrow of love
And made me one with the Lord who made me.
This is the only love I have to prove,
And my life is so completely transformed
That my Beloved One has become mine
And without a doubt I am his at last.

Her Heart Is Full of Joy

Her heart is full of joy with love,
For in the Lord her mind is stilled.
She has renounced every selfish attachment
And draws abiding joy and strength
From the One within.
She lives not for herself, but lives
To serve the Lord of Love in all,
And swims across the sea of life
Breasting its rough waves joyfully.

As the rivers flowing east and west

    merge in the sea and become one with it,

    forgetting they were ever separate streams,

    so do all creatures lose their separateness

    when they merge at last into pure Being.

    —THE CHANDOGYA UPANISHAD

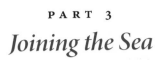

PART 3

Joining the Sea

Invocations

1

Lead me from the unreal to the real.
Lead me from darkness to light.
Lead me from death to immortality.

2

O M
With our ears may we hear what is good.
With our eyes may we behold thy righteousness.
Tranquil in body, may we who worship thee find rest.
   O M *shanti shanti shanti*
   O M . . . Hail to the supreme Self!

3

May my speech be one with my mind,
   and may my mind be one with my speech.
O thou self-luminous Brahman,
   remove the veil of ignorance from before me,
   that I may behold thy light.
Do thou reveal to me the spirit of the scriptures.
May the truth of the scriptures be ever present to me.
May I seek day and night to realize
   what I learn from the sages.
May I speak the truth of Brahman.
May I speak the truth.
May it protect me.
May it protect my teacher.

God Makes the Rivers to Flow

God makes the rivers to flow. They tire not, nor
do they cease from flowing. May the river of my
life flow into the sea of love that is the Lord.

May I overcome all the impediments in my course.
May the thread of my song be not cut before my
life merges in the sea of love.

Guard me against all danger, O Lord. Accept me
graciously, O King of kings.

Release me from my sorrows, which hold me as
ropes hold a calf. I cannot even open my eyes
without the power of your love.

Guard us against the grief that haunts the life
of the selfish. Lead us from darkness into light.

We will sing of your love as it was sung of
old. Your laws change not, but stand like the
mountains.

Forgive me all the mistakes I have committed.
Many mornings will dawn upon us again. Guide
us through them all, O Lord of Love.

I Am the Resurrection & the Life

I am the resurrection and the life, saith the Lord;
He that believeth in me, though he were dead, yet shall he live;
    and whosoever liveth and believeth in me shall never die.

None of us liveth to himself, and no man dieth to himself.
    For if we live, we live unto the Lord,
    and if we die, we die unto the Lord.
Whether we live, therefore, or die, we are the Lord's.

The eternal God is thy refuge, and underneath are the
    everlasting arms.

God is our hope and strength, a very present help in trouble.
Therefore will we not fear, though the earth be moved,
    and though the hills be carried into the midst of the sea;
Though the waters thereof rage and swell,
    and though the mountains shake at the tempest of the same.

There is a river, the streams whereof make glad the city of God,
    the holy place of the tabernacle of the Most Highest.
God is in the midst of her, therefore shall she not be removed.

Be still then, and know that I am God.

Lord, thou hast been our refuge
    from one generation to another.
Before the mountains were brought forth,
    or ever the earth and the world were made,
Thou art God from everlasting, and the world without end.
For a thousand years in thy sight are but as yesterday
when it is past, and as a watch in the night.

Neither death, nor life, nor angels, nor principalities, nor powers,
    nor things present, nor things to come,
    nor height, nor depth, nor any other creature,
shall be able to separate us from the love of God.

Our light affliction, which is but for a moment,
worketh for us a far more exceeding and eternal weight of glory;
While we do not look at the things which are seen,
    but at the things which are not seen:
For the things which are seen are temporal,
    but the things which are not seen are eternal.

We know that if our earthly house of this tabernacle
    were dissolved, we have a building of God,
    a house not made with hands, eternal in the heavens.

I Come to Him Running

The Prophet said,

God Most High has said:
When my worshipper's thoughts turn to Me,
    there am I with him.
And when he makes mention of Me within himself,
    I make mention of him within Myself:
and when he makes mention of Me in company,
    I make mention of him in a better company.
If he draw near to Me a hand's breadth,
    I draw near to him an arm's length;
and if he draw near to me an arm's length,
    I draw near to him the length of both arms
    wide outstretched;
and if he come to Me walking, I come to him running.
And if he meet Me with sins equivalent to the whole world,
    I will greet him with forgiveness equal to it.

All Paths Lead to Me

He who knows me as his own divine Self,
As the Operator in him, breaks through
The belief he is the body, and is
Not born separate again. Such a one
Is united with me, O Arjuna.

Delivered from selfish attachment, fear,
And anger, filled with Me, surrendering
Themselves to me, purified in the fire
Of my Being, many have reached the
State of Unity in me.

As people approach me, so I receive
Them. All paths lead to me, O Arjuna.

The Blessing of a Well-Trained Mind

As an archer aims his arrow, the wise aim their restless thoughts, hard to aim, hard to restrain.

As a fish hooked and left on the sand thrashes about in agony, the mind being trained in meditation trembles all over, desperate to escape the hand of Mara the Tempter.

Hard it is to train the mind, which goes where it likes and does what it wants. But a trained mind brings health and happiness. The wise can direct their thoughts, subtle and elusive, wherever they choose: a trained mind brings health and happiness. Those who can direct thoughts, which are unsubstantial and wander so aimlessly, are freed from the bonds of Mara.

They are not wise whose thoughts are not steady and minds not serene, who do not know dharma, the law of life. They are wise whose thoughts are steady and minds serene, unaffected by good and bad. They are awake and free from fear.

Remember, this body is like a fragile clay pot. Make your mind a fortress and conquer Mara with the weapon of wisdom. Guard your conquest always.

More than those who hate you, more than all your enemies, an untrained mind does greater harm. More than your mother, more than your father, more than all your family, a well-trained mind does greater good.

Mourner's Kaddish

May His great Name grow exalted and sanctified
   in the world that He created as He willed.
May He give reign to His kingship in your lifetimes
     and in your days,
     and in the lifetimes of the entire Family of Israel,
     swiftly and soon.

May His great Name be blessed forever and ever.
Blessed, praised, glorified, exalted, extolled,
     mighty, upraised, and lauded be the Name
       of the Holy One,
     Blessed is He beyond any blessing and song,
     praise, and consolation that are uttered in the world.

May there be abundant peace from Heaven, and life
   upon us and upon all Israel.

He Who makes peace in the heights, may He make peace
   upon us and upon all Israel.

Adon Olam

The Lord of the universe
Ruled before creation.
When by his will all things came to be,
The name of the Lord was known.
As the Lord creates, he may end the creation,
Remaining alone, unmanifested.
He was, he is, and he shall remain eternal.
He is without beginning;
He is without end.
He is my God, my living strength,
My refuge when I grieve.
He is my only desire.
I live in him alone.
My soul abides in his hands
In sleep as in wakefulness.
Though I leave my body
I will not fear,
For the Lord is with my soul.

Great Life-Giving Spirit

Great Spirit of love, come to me with the power of the North.
Make me courageous when the cold winds of life fall upon me.

Give me strength and endurance for everything
that is harsh, everything that hurts,
everything that makes me squint.
Make me move through life
ready to take what comes from the North.

Spirit who comes out of the East,
come to me with the power of the rising sun.
Let there be light in my word.
Let there be light on the path that I walk.
Let me remember always that you give the gift of a new day.
Never let me be burdened with sorrow by not starting over.

Great Spirit of creation,
send me the warm and soothing winds from the South.
Comfort me and caress me when I am tired and cold.
Enfold me as your gentle breezes enfold your leaves
    on the trees.
And as you give to all the earth your warm, moving wind,
Give to me so that I may grow close to you in warmth.

Great life-giving Spirit,
I face the West,
the direction of the sundown.
Let me remember every day that the moment will come
when my sun will go down.
Never let me forget that I must fade into you.
Give me beautiful color.
Give me a great sky for setting,
and when it is time to meet you,
I come with glory.

And Giver of all life, I pray to you from the earth,
help me to remember as I touch the earth
that I am little and need your pity.
Help me to be thankful for the gift of the earth
and never to walk hurtfully on the world.
Bless me to love what comes from mother earth
and teach me how to love your gifts.

Great Spirit of the heavens,
lift me up to you
that my heart may worship you
and come to you in glory.
Hold in my memory that you are my Creator,
greater than I,
eager for my good life.
Let everything that is in the world
lift my mind,
and my heart,
and my life to you
so that we may come always to you
in truth and in heart.

Great Life-Giving Spirit

Let Me Walk in Beauty

O Great Spirit,
whose voice I hear in the winds
and whose breath gives life to all the world,
hear me.
I am small and weak.
I need your strength and wisdom.

Let me walk in beauty
and let my eyes ever behold the red and purple sunset.
Make my hands respect the things you have made
and my ears grow sharp to hear your voice.

Make me wise so that I may understand the things
you have taught my people.
Let me learn the lessons you have hidden
in every leaf and rock.
I seek strength not to be greater than my brother or
sister
but to fight my greatest enemy, myself.
Make me always ready
to come to you with clean hands and straight eyes
So when life fades as the fading sunset
my spirit may come to you without shame.

What Is Real Never Ceases

The Self dwells in the house of the body,
Which passes through childhood, youth, and old age.
So passes the Self at the time of death
Into another body. The wise know this truth
And are not deceived by it.

When the senses come in contact with sense-objects
They give rise to feelings of heat and cold,
Pleasure and pain, which come and go.
Accept them calmly, as do the wise.

The wise, who live free from pleasure and pain,
Are worthy of immortality.

What is real never ceases to be.
The unreal never is. The sages
Who realize the Self know the secret
Of what is and what is not.

Know that the Self, the ground of existence,
Can never be destroyed or diminished.
For the changeless cannot be changed.

Bodies die, not the Self that dwells therein.
Know the Self to be beyond change and death.
Therefore strive to realize this Self.

Those who look upon the Self as slayer
Or as slain have not realized the Self.
How can the Self be killed or kill
When there is only One?

Never was the Self born; never shall it
Cease to be. Without beginning or end,
Free from birth, free from death, and free from time,
How can the Self die when the body dies?

Who knows the Self to be birthless, deathless,
Not subject to the tyranny of time,
How can the Self slay or cause to be slain?

Even as we cast off worn-out garments
And put on new ones, so casts off the Self
A worn-out body and enters into
Another that is new.

Not pierced by arrows nor burnt by fire,
Affected by neither water nor wind,
The Self is not a physical creature.

Not wounded, not burnt, not wetted, not dried,
The Self is ever and everywhere,
Immovable and everlasting.

The Self cannot be known by the senses,
Nor thought by the mind, nor caught by time.
If you know this, you will not grieve.

Even if you mistake the Self to be
Subject to birth and death, you must not grieve.
For death is certain for those who are born,
As rebirth is certain for those who die.
Why grieve over what cannot be avoided?

What Is Real Never Ceases

We perceive creatures only after birth,
And after they die we perceive them not.
They are manifest only between birth
And death. In this there is no cause for grief.

Some there are who have realized the Self
In all its wonder. Others can speak of it
As wonderful. But there are many
Who don't understand even when they hear.

Deathless is the Self in every creature.
Know this truth, and leave all sorrow behind.

The One Appearing as Many

May the Lord of Love, who projects himself
Into the universe of myriad forms
Through maya, from whom all beings come,
To whom all beings finally return,
May he grant us the grace of wisdom.

He is the fire and the sun, and the moon
And the stars. He is the air and the sea,
And the creator Prajapati.

He is this boy, he is that girl; he is
This man, he is that woman, and he is
This old man, too, tottering on his staff.
His face is seen everywhere.

He is the blue bird, he is the green bird
With red eyes; he is the thundercloud, and
He is the seasons and the seas; he has
No beginning, he has no end. He is
The source from whom all the worlds evolve.

From his divine power of maya comes
Forth this magical show of name and form,
Of you and me, which casts the spell of pain
And pleasure. When we pierce through the magic,
We see the One who appears as many.

Two birds of beautiful plumage, comrades
Inseparable, live on the same tree.
One bird eats the fruit of pleasure and pain;
The other looks on without eating.

Forgetting our divine origin, we
Become ensnared in the world of maya
And bewail our helplessness. But when we
See the Lord of Love in all his glory,
Adored by all, we go beyond sorrow.

What use are the scriptures to anyone
Who knows not the one source from whom they come,
In whom all gods and worlds abide? Only
They who realize him as ever present
In their hearts attain abiding joy.

The Lord, who is the supreme magician,
Brings forth out of himself all the scriptures,
Oblations, sacrifices, spiritual
Disciplines, past and present, and the whole
Universe. Though he is not visible,
He remains hidden in the hearts of all.

Know him to be the supreme magician
Who has brought all the worlds out of himself.
Know that all beings in the universe
Partake of his divine splendor.

Know him to be the supreme magician
Who has become boy and girl, bird and beast.
He is the bestower of all blessings,
And his grace fills the heart with peace profound.

Know him to be the supreme source of all
The gods, support of the universe,
And sower of the golden seed of life.
May he grant us the grace of wisdom.

Know him to be the supreme God of gods,
From whom all the worlds draw their breath of life.
He rules every creature from within.
May he be worshipped by everyone.

Know him to be the supreme pervader,
In whom the whole universe is smaller
Than the smallest atom. May he, Shiva,
Fill our heart with infinite peace.

Know him to be the supreme guardian
Of the cosmos, protecting all creatures
From within. May he, Shiva, in whom all
Are one, free us from the bonds of death.

Know him to be the Supreme One, hidden
In the hearts of all as cream is in milk
And yet encompassing the universe.
May he, Shiva, free us from all bondage.

Know him to be the supreme architect
Who is enshrined in the hearts of all.
Know him in the depths of meditation.
May he grant us immortality.

Know him to be the supreme source of all
Religions, ruler of the world of light,
Where there is neither day nor night, neither
What is nor what is not, but only Shiva.
He is beyond the reach of the mind.
He alone is. His glory fills all worlds.

The One Appearing as Many

He is beyond the reach of the eye.
He alone is. May he, Shiva, reveal
Himself in the depths of meditation
And grant us immortality.

I live in fear of death, O Lord of Love;
I seek refuge at your feet. Protect me,
Protect us, man and woman, cow and horse.
May the brave ones who seek you be released
From the bondage of death.

ॐ

Lord That Giveth Strength

1

My child, I am the Lord, that giveth strength in the day of tribulation. Come thou unto me, when it is not well with thee.

This is that which most of all hindereth heavenly consolation, that thou art too slow in turning thyself unto prayer.

For before thou dost earnestly supplicate me, thou seekest in the meanwhile many comforts, and refreshest thyself in outward things.

And hence it comes to pass that all doth little profit thee, until thou well consider that I am he who do rescue them that trust in me; and that out of me there is neither powerful help, nor profitable counsel, nor lasting remedy.

But do thou, having now recovered breath after the tempest, gather strength again in the light of my mercies; for I am at hand (saith the Lord) to repair all, not only entirely, but also abundantly and in most plentiful measure.

2

Is there anything hard to me? Or shall I be like one that saith and doeth not?

Where is thy faith? Stand firmly and with perseverance; take courage and be patient; comfort will come to thee in due time. Wait, wait, I say, for me: I will come and take care of thee.

It is a temptation that vexeth thee, and a vain fear that affrighteth thee.

What else doth anxiety about future contingencies bring thee, but sorrow upon sorrow? Sufficient for the day is the evil thereof.

It is a vain thing and unprofitable to be either disturbed or pleased about future things, which perhaps will never come to pass.

3

But it is incident to man to be deluded with such imaginations; and a sign of a mind as yet weak to be so easily drawn away by the suggestions of the Enemy.

For so he may delude and deceive thee, he careth not whether it be by true or by false propositions; nor whether he overthrows thee with the love of present, or the fear of future things.

Let not therefore thy heart be troubled, neither let it fear. Trust in me, and put thy confidence in my mercy.

When thou thinkest thyself farthest off from me, oftentimes I am nearest unto thee.

When thou countest almost all to be lost, then oftentimes the greatest gain of reward is close at hand. All is not lost, when any thing falleth out contrary.

Thou oughtest not to judge according to present feeling; nor so to take any grief, or give thyself over to it, from whencesoever it cometh, as though all hopes of escape were quite taken away.

4

Think not thyself wholly left, although for a time I have sent thee some tribulation, or even have withdrawn thy desired comfort; for this is the way to the kingdom of heaven.

Lord That Giveth Strength

And without doubt it is more expedient for thee and the rest of my servants that ye be exercised with adversities, than that ye should have all things according to your desires.

I know the secret thoughts of thy heart, and that it is very expedient for thy welfare that thou be left sometimes without taste (of spiritual sweetness, and in a dry condition), lest perhaps thou shouldest be puffed up with thy prosperous estate, and shouldest be willing to please thyself in that which thou art not.

That which I have given, I can take away; and I can restore it again when I please.

When I give it, it is mine; when I withdraw it, I take not any thing that is thine; for mine is every good gift and every perfect gift.

If I send upon thee affliction, or any cross whatever, repine not, nor let thy heart fail thee; I can quickly succor thee, and turn all thy heaviness into joy.

Howbeit I am righteous, and greatly to be praised when I deal thus with thee.

5

If thou art wise, and considerest what the truth is, thou never oughtest to mourn dejectedly for any adversity that befalleth thee, but rather to rejoice and give thanks.

Yea, thou wilt account this time especial joy, that I afflict thee with sorrows, and do not spare thee.

As the Father hath loved me, I also love you, said I unto my beloved disciples; whom certainly I sent not out to temporal joys, but to great conflicts; not to honors, but to contempts; not to idleness, but to labors; not to rest, but to bring forth much fruit with patience. Remember thou these words, O my child!

Four Things That Bring Much Inward Peace

My child, now will I teach thee the way of peace and true liberty.

O Lord, I beseech thee, do as thou sayest, for this is delightful for me to hear.

Be desirous, my child, to work for the welfare of another rather than seek thine own will.

Choose always to have less rather than more.

Seek always the lowest place, and to be inferior to everyone.

Wish always, and pray, that the will of God may be wholly fulfilled in thee.

Behold, such a man entereth within the borders of peace and rest.

O Lord, this short discourse of thine containeth within itself much perfection. It is little to be spoken, but full of meaning, and abundant in fruit. . . . Thou who canst do all things, and ever lovest the profiting of my soul, increase in me thy grace, that I may be able to fulfill thy words, and to work out mine own salvation.

The Island

For those struggling in midstream,
　　in great fear of the flood,
　　of growing old and of dying –
for all those I say, an island exists
　　where there is no place for impediments,
　　no place for clinging:
the island of no going beyond.

I call it nirvana,
　　the complete destruction
　　of old age and dying.

☙

The Lord Is My Shepherd

The Lord is my shepherd; I shall not want.

He maketh me to lie down in green pastures;
　　He leadeth me beside the still waters.

He restoreth my soul; He guideth me in straight paths
　　for His name's sake.

Yea, though I walk through the valley
　　of the shadow of death,
　　I will fear no evil, for Thou art with me;
　　Thy rod and Thy staff, they comfort me.

Thou preparest a table before me
　　in the presence of mine enemies;
　　Thou hast anointed my head with oil;
　　my cup runneth over.

Surely goodness and mercy shall follow me
　　all the days of my life;
　　and I shall dwell in the house of the Lord for ever.

The Path

I know the path: it is strait and narrow.
It is like the edge of a sword.

I rejoice to walk on it.
I weep when I slip.

God's word is:
"He who strives never perishes."

I have implicit faith in that promise.

Though, therefore, from my weakness
I fail a thousand times,
I shall not lose faith.

In the Midst of Darkness

I do dimly perceive that whilst everything around me is ever changing, ever dying, there is underlying all that change a living power that is changeless, that holds all together, that creates, dissolves, and re-creates. That informing power or spirit is God. And since nothing else that I see merely through the senses can or will persist, He alone is.

And is this power benevolent or malevolent? I see it as purely benevolent. For I can see that in the midst of death life persists, in the midst of untruth truth persists, in the midst of darkness light persists. Hence I gather that God is Life, Truth, Light. He is Love. He is the Supreme Good.

That Wondrous Star

She is truly like a star,

That noble star of Jacob
    whose rays illumine the universe,
    shine in the highest heaven,
    penetrate the darkest depths,
    and spread throughout the earth,
    warming goodness like springtime,
    burning out evil.

She is that bright and wondrous star
    forever raised above the great wide sea
    of this world, sparkling with merit,
    a shining guide.

O voyager, whoever you may be,
    when you find yourself in stormy seas
    in danger of foundering in the tempests
    and far from land, lest you sink and drown,
    fix your eyes on this bright star; call out to Mary.

When temptations blow
    or the shoals of tribulation threaten,
    fix your eyes on this star; call out to Mary.

When the waves of pride or ambition batter your soul,
    of slander or jealousy, anger or lust,
    fix your eyes on this star; call out to Mary.

In doubt, in danger, in precarious straits,
    fix your mind on Mary; call out to Mary.
Never let her leave you, keep her with you always,
    "even in thy mouth and in thy heart."
Never abandon her presence, never leave her company,
    to win approval in her prayers.

Follow her and you will never lose your way.
Appeal to her and you will never lose hope.
Think of her always and you will never stray.
With her holding you, you cannot fall.
With her protection, you cannot fear.
When she leads, you cannot tire.
With her grace you will come safely
    through to journey's end.
Then you will know for yourself
    why she bears the name "Star of the Sea."

Let Nothing Upset You

Let nothing upset you;
Let nothing frighten you.
Everything is changing;
God alone is changeless.
Patience attains the goal.
Who has God lacks nothing;
God alone fills every need.

Do Not Look with Fear

Do not look with fear
    on the changes and chances of this life;
    rather look to them with full faith that as they arise,
    God – whose you are – will deliver you out of them.

He has kept you hitherto.
Do not but hold fast to His dear hand,
    and He will lead you safely through all things;
    and when you cannot stand, He will bear you
    in His arms.

Do not anticipate what will happen tomorrow.
The same everlasting Father who cares for you today
    will take care of you tomorrow and every day.
Either He will shield you from suffering or
    He will give you unfailing strength to bear it.

Be at peace, then, and put aside all anxious thoughts
    and imaginations.

The One Thing Needed

Of what avail this restless, hurrying activity?
This heavy weight of earthly duties?

God's purposes stand firm,
And thou, His little one,
Needest one thing alone:
Trust in His power, and will, to meet thy need.

Thy burden resteth safe on Him,
And thou, His little one,
Mayst play securely at His side.

This is the sum and substance of it all:
God is,
God loveth thee,
God beareth all thy care.

Soul of My Soul

You are the soul of my soul,
your energy my wisdom and mind;
my body is your abode,
my sensory enjoyment an oblation to you.
My powers and desires join with your will;
my life an instrument of your purpose.
My every word joins hymns to you.
I walk each step as pilgrimage to your shrine.

Errors by my hand or foot,
by my speech, or body,
by my ears, eyes, or thought;
whether by what I've done or failed to do,
dear Lord, forgive all these.
O ocean of mercy, God of gods,
bestower of blissful peace,
victory unto you!

The Eternal Godhead

Those who remember me at the time of death will come to me. Do not doubt this. Whatever occupies the mind at the time of death determines the destination of the dying; always they will tend toward that state of being. Therefore, remember me at all times and fight on. With your heart and mind intent on me, you will surely come to me. When you make your mind one-pointed through regular practice of meditation, you will find the supreme glory of the Lord.

The Lord is the supreme poet, the first cause, the sovereign ruler, subtler than the tiniest particle, the support of all, inconceivable, bright as the sun, beyond darkness. Remembering him in this way at the time of death, through devotion and the power of meditation, with your mind completely stilled and your concentration fixed in the center of spiritual awareness between the eyebrows, you will realize the supreme Lord.

I will tell you briefly of the eternal state all scriptures affirm, which can be entered only by those who are self-controlled and free from selfish passions. Those whose lives are dedicated to Brahman attain this supreme goal.

Remembering me at the time of death, close down the doors of the senses and place the mind in the heart. Then, while absorbed in meditation, focus all energy upwards to the head. Repeating in this state the divine Name, the syllable O M that represents the changeless Brahman, you will go forth from the body and attain the supreme goal.

I am easily attained by the person who always remembers me and is attached to nothing else. Such a person is a true yogi, Arjuna. Great souls make their lives perfect and discover me; they are freed from mortality and the suffering of this separate existence. Every creature in the universe is subject to rebirth, Arjuna, except the one who is united with me.

The Immortal

There is a city with eleven gates
Of which the ruler is the unborn Self,
Whose light forever shines.
They go beyond sorrow who meditate on the Self
And are freed from the cycle of birth and death.
For this Self is supreme!

The Self is the sun shining in the sky,
The wind blowing in space; he is the fire
At the altar and in the home the guest;
He dwells in human beings, in gods, in truth,
And in the vast firmament; he is the fish
Born in water, the plant growing in the earth,
The river flowing down from the mountain.
For this Self is supreme!

The adorable one who is seated
In the heart rules the breath of life.
Unto him all the senses pay their homage.
When the dweller in the body breaks out
In freedom from the bonds of flesh, what remains?
For this Self is supreme!
We live not by the breath that flows in
And flows out, but by him who causes the breath
To flow in and flow out.

Now, O Nachiketa, I will tell you
Of this unseen, eternal Brahman, and
What befalls the Self after death.
Of those unaware of the Self, some are born
As embodied creatures while others remain
In a lower stage of evolution,
As determined by their own need for growth.

That which is awake even in our sleep,
Giving form in dreams to the objects of
Sense craving, that indeed is pure light,
Brahman the immortal, who contains all
The cosmos, and beyond whom none can go.
For this Self is supreme!

As the same fire assumes different shapes
When it consumes objects differing in shape,
So does the one Self take the shape
Of every creature in whom he is present.
As the same air assumes different shapes
When it enters objects differing in shape,
So does the one Self take the shape
Of every creature in whom he is present.

As the sun, who is the eye of the world,
Cannot be tainted by the defects in our eyes
Or by the objects it looks on,
So the one Self, dwelling in all, cannot
Be tainted by the evils of the world.
For this Self transcends all!

The ruler supreme, inner Self of all,
Multiplies his oneness into many.
Eternal joy is theirs who see the Self
In their own hearts. To none else does it come!
Changeless amidst the things that pass away,

Pure consciousness in all who are conscious,
The One answers the prayers of many.
Eternal peace is theirs who see the Self
In their own hearts. To none else does it come!

NACHIKETA:

How can I know that blissful Self, supreme,
Inexpressible, realized by the wise?
Is he the light, or does he reflect light?

THE KING OF DEATH:

There shines not the sun, neither moon nor star,
Nor flash of lightning, nor fire lit on earth.
The Self is the light reflected by all.
He shining, everything shines after him.

The Power of the Holy Name

If you want to know the power
Of the holy name of Rama,
Spend your time with lovers of God.

To repeat the name constantly
May be hard and bitter at first,
But don't stop until it becomes sweet
Like the luscious mango to the taste.

When the time comes for the body
To be shed, the name of Rama
Will take you safely through death's door.
So keep singing *Rama, Rama*
In your mind, and the Lord of Love
Will take you safely from this shore
Of death to immortality.

Even with Your Last Breath

Even with your last breath
Repeat the name of the Lord,
Whose abode stands high like a date palm,
Loaded with luscious fruits.

Do not depend on your own
Skill and strength to reach the top.

Let the Holy Name be your ladder and your rope.
Thus supported you can neither
Fall nor fail to reach the top.

Make this house of flesh and blood
A temple of the Lord.
This is Meera's secret to share with you.

Singing Your Name

Singing your name day and night,
It echoes in my mind all the time.
O Krishna, I am the dust of your feet;
How can I lift my voice in your praise?

Singing your name heals all wounds,
And guards the mind against selfish thoughts.

I am armed with the arrow of your name
Fixed on the bow-string of my heart;
I wear the armor of your glory
As I sing of your life and divine deeds.

My body is a musical instrument
On which my mind plays songs of love.

To awaken my soul from sleep,
I sing and dance before the Lord
Waiting for the door to open.

Think on His Name

Whilst thou art busy at work,
Think on His name:

Then shall evil be vanquished,
And grief shall be turned into peace:

To this at the end thou must come,
When thy last breath faileth,
And home, children, wealth, are forgotten:

For long thou canst put Him off,
Thou canst live thy life as thou wilt,
But at last thy barque shall be sucked
    to the whirlpool:

Break the snares from thee now,
Do now what thou some day must do:

At the end thou hast one defense,
One only,
Trust in His name.
By this alone thou canst find salvation,
But by this alone:

Then trust in Him now.

How Great Is His Name!

If you would have peace,
Seek it in His name.
If you want to see God,
Chant His holy name.
If you wish for freedom and joy,
Find it in His name.
If you aspire for life eternal,
On your tongue have His name.
Name is your path,
Name is your goal;
Name is the means,
Name is the end.
Name is the Truth,
Name is God.

O Name, Stream Down in Moonlight

Chant the Name of the Lord and his glory unceasingly,
That the mirror of the heart may be wiped clean
And quenched that mighty forest fire,
Worldly lust, raging furiously within.

O Name, stream down in moonlight on the lotus heart,
Opening its cup to knowledge of thyself.
O self, drown deep in the waves of his bliss,
Chanting his Name continually,
Tasting his nectar at every step,
Bathing in his Name, that bath for weary souls.
In each and every Name thy power resides.
No times are set, no rites are needful,
For chanting of thy Name,
So vast is thy mercy.

Weaving Your Name

I weave your name on the loom of my mind,
To make my garment when you come to me.
My loom has ten thousand threads
To make my garment when you come to me.
The sun and moon watch while I weave your name;
The sun and moon hear while I count your name.
These are the wages I get by day and night
To deposit in the lotus bank of my heart.

I weave your name on the loom of my mind
To clean and soften ten thousand threads
And to comb the twists and knots of my thoughts.
No more shall I weave a garment of pain.
For you have come to me, drawn by my weaving –
My ceaselessly weaving your name
    on the loom of my mind.

Chant the Sweet Name of God

With beaming face chant the sweet name of God
Till in your heart the nectar overflows.
Drink of it ceaselessly and share it with all!
If ever your heart runs dry, parched by the flames
Of worldly desire, chant the sweet name of God,
And heavenly love will moisten your arid soul.

Be sure, O mind, you never forget to chant
His holy name: when danger stares in your face,
Call on Him, your Father Compassionate;
With His name's thunder, snap the fetters of sin!
Come, let us fulfill our hearts' desires
By drinking deep of Everlasting Joy,
Made one with Him in Love's pure ecstasy.

Thy Holy Name

I do not ask Thee, Mother,
Riches, good fortune, or salvation;
I seek no happiness, no knowledge.
This is my only prayer to Thee:
That as the breath of my life forsakes me,
I may chant Thy holy name.

You Are That

This is the teaching of Uddalaka to Shvetaketu, his son:

As by knowing one lump of clay, dear one,
We come to know all things made out of clay –
That they differ only in name and form,
While the stuff of which all are made is clay;

As by knowing one gold nugget, dear one,
We come to know all things made out of gold –
That they differ only in name and form,
While the stuff of which all are made is gold;

As by knowing one tool of iron, dear one,
We come to know all things made out of iron –
That they differ only in name and form,
While the stuff of which all are made is iron –

So through spiritual wisdom, dear one,
We come to know that all of life is one.

In the beginning was only Being,
One without a second.
Out of himself he brought forth the cosmos
And entered into everything in it.
There is nothing that does not come from him.
Of everything he is the inmost Self.
He is the truth; he is the Self supreme.
You are that, Shvetaketu; you are that.

When a person is absorbed in dreamless sleep
He is one with the Self, though he knows it not.
We say he sleeps, but he sleeps in the Self.
As a tethered bird grows tired of flying
About in vain to find a place of rest
And settles down at last on its own perch,
So the mind, tired of wandering about
Hither and thither, settles down at last
In the Self, dear one, to whom it is bound.
All creatures, dear one, have their source in him.
He is their home; he is their strength.
There is nothing that does not come from him.
Of everything he is the inmost Self.
He is the truth; he is the Self supreme.
You are that, Shvetaketu; you are that.

As bees suck nectar from many a flower
And make their honey one, so that no drop
Can say, "I am from this flower or that,"
All creatures, though one, know not they are that One.
There is nothing that does not come from him.
Of everything he is the inmost Self.
He is the truth; he is the Self supreme.
You are that, Shvetaketu; you are that.

As the rivers flowing east and west
Merge in the sea and become one with it,
Forgetting they were ever separate streams,
So do all creatures lose their separateness
When they merge at last into pure Being.
There is nothing that does not come from him.
Of everything he is the inmost Self.
He is the truth; he is the Self supreme.
You are that, Shvetaketu; you are that!

A Sea of Peace

When the good God calls us in this world, he finds us full of vices and sins, and his first work is to give us the instinct to practice virtue; then he incites us to desire perfection, and afterwards, by infused grace, he conducts us to the true self-naughting, and finally to the true transformation. This is the extraordinary road along which God conducts the soul. But when the soul is thus naughted and transformed, it no longer works, or speaks, or wills, or feels, or understands, nor has it in itself any knowledge, either of that which is internal or external, which could possibly affect it; and, in all these things God is its director and guide without the help of any creature.

In this state, the soul is in such peace and tranquility that it seems to her that both soul and body are immersed in a sea of the profoundest peace, from which she would not issue for anything that could happen in this life. She remains immovable, imperturbable, and neither her humanity nor her spirit feels anything except the sweetest peace, of which she is so full that if her flesh, her bones, her nerves were pressed, nothing would issue from them but peace. And all day long she sings softly to herself for joy, saying: *"Shall I show thee what God is? No one finds peace apart from him."*

The Tree of Eternity

The Tree of Eternity has its roots above
And its branches on earth below.
Its pure root is Brahman the immortal,
From whom all the worlds draw their life, and whom
None can transcend. For this Self is supreme!

The cosmos comes forth from Brahman and moves
In him. With his power it reverberates,
Like thunder crashing in the sky. Those who realize him
Pass beyond the sway of death.

In fear of him fire burns; in fear of him
The sun shines, the clouds rain, and the winds blow.
In fear of him death stalks about to kill.

If one fails to realize Brahman in this life
Before the physical sheath is shed,
He must again put on a body
In the world of embodied creatures.

Brahman can be seen, as in a mirror,
In a pure heart; in the world of the ancestors
As in a dream; in the gandharva world
As the reflections in trembling waters;
And clear as light in the realm of the Creator.

Knowing the senses to be separate
From the Self, and the sense experience
To be fleeting, the wise grieve no more.

Above the senses is the mind,
Above the mind is the intellect, above that
Is the ego, and above the ego
Is the unmanifested Cause.
And beyond is Brahman, omnipresent,
Attributeless. Realizing him one is released
From the cycle of birth and death.

He is formless, and can never be seen
With these two eyes. But he reveals himself
In the heart made pure through meditation
And sense-restraint. Realizing him one is released
From the cycle of birth and death.

When the five senses are stilled, when the mind
Is stilled, when the intellect is stilled,
That is called the highest state by the wise.
They say yoga is this complete stillness
In which one enters the unitive state,
Never to become separate again.
If one is not established in this state,
The sense of unity will come and go.

The unitive state cannot be attained
Through words or thoughts or through the eye.
How can it be attained except through one who is
Established in this state himself?

There are two selves, the separate ego
And the indivisible Atman.
When one rises above I, me, and mine,
The Atman is revealed as one's real Self.

When all desires that surge in the heart
Are renounced, the mortal becomes immortal.
When all the knots that strangle the heart
Are loosened, the mortal becomes immortal.
This sums up the teaching of the scriptures.

From the heart there radiate a hundred
And one vital tracks. One of them rises
To the crown of the head. This way leads
To immortality, the others to death.

The Lord of Love, not larger than the thumb,
Is ever enshrined in the hearts of all.
Draw him clear out of the physical sheath,
As one draws the stalk from the munja grass.
Know thyself to be pure and immortal!
Know thyself to be pure and immortal!

SAINT AUGUSTINE
Entering into Joy

Imagine if all the tumult of the body were to quiet down,
along with all our busy thoughts about earth, sea, and air;
if the very world should stop, and the mind cease thinking
about itself, go beyond itself, and be quite still;

if all the fantasies that appear in dreams and imagination
should cease, and there be no speech, no sign:

Imagine if all things that are perishable grew still – for if we
listen they are saying, *We did not make ourselves; he made us
who abides forever* – imagine, then, that they should say this
and fall silent, listening to the very voice of him who made
them and not to that of his creation;

so that we should hear not his word through the tongues of
men, nor the voice of angels, nor the clouds' thunder, nor any
symbol, but the very Self which in these things we love, and
go beyond ourselves to attain a flash of that eternal wisdom
which abides above all things:

And imagine if that moment were to go on and on, leaving
behind all other sights and sounds but this one vision which
ravishes and absorbs and fixes the beholder in joy; so that
the rest of eternal life were like that moment of illumination
which leaves us breathless:

Would this not be what is bidden in scripture,
Enter thou into the joy of thy lord?

Thou One without a Second

Oh, when will dawn for me that day of blessedness
When He who is all Good, all Beauty, and all Truth
Will light the inmost shrine of my heart?
When shall I sink at last, ever beholding Him,
Into that Ocean of Delight?
Lord, as Infinite Wisdom Thou shalt enter my soul,
And my unquiet mind, made speechless by Thy sight,
Will find a haven at Thy feet.
In my heart's firmament, O Lord, Thou wilt arise
As Blissful Immortality;
And as, when the chakora beholds the rising moon,
It sports about for very joy,
So, too, shall I be filled with heavenly happiness
When Thou appearest unto me.

Thou One without a Second, all Peace, the King of Kings!
At Thy beloved feet I shall renounce my life
And so at last shall gain life's goal;
I shall enjoy the bliss of heaven while yet on earth!
Where else is a boon so rare bestowed?
Then shall I see Thy glory, pure and untouched by stain;
As darkness flees from light, so will my darkest sins
Desert me at Thy dawn's approach.
Kindle in me, O Lord, the blazing fire of faith
To be the pole-star of my life;
O Succour of the weak, fulfil my one desire!
Then shall I bathe both day and night
In the boundless bliss of Thy Love, and utterly forget
Myself, O Lord, attaining Thee.

Love the Lord & Be Free

To know the unity of all life leads
To deathlessness; to know not leads to death.
Both are hidden in the infinity
Of Brahman, who is beyond both.

He is the One who presides over all
And rules over everyone from within.
He sows the golden seed of life when time begins
And helps us know its unity.

He is the Lord who casts the net of birth
And death and withdraws it again,
The supreme Self who governs the forces of life.

Even as the sun shines and fills all space
With light, above, below, across, so shines the Lord
Of Love and fills the hearts of all created beings.

From him the cosmos comes, who teaches
Each living creature to attain perfection
According to its own nature. He is
The Lord of Love who reigns over all life.

He is the supreme creator, hidden
Deep in the mystery of the scriptures.
By realizing him the gods and sages
Attained immortality.

Under the hypnotic spell of pleasure
And pain, we live for ourselves and are bound.
Though master of ourselves, we roam about
From birth to birth, driven by our own deeds.

The Self, small as the thumb, dwelling in the heart,
Is like the sun shining in the sky.
But when identified with the ego,
The Self appears other than what it is.

It may appear smaller than a hair's breadth,
But know the Self to be infinite.
Not female, male, nor neuter is the Self.
As is the body, so is the gender.

The Self takes on a body, with desires,
Attachments, and delusions. The Self
Is born again and again in new bodies
To work out the karma of former lives.

The embodied self assumes many forms,
Heavy or light, according to its needs
For growth and the deeds of previous lives.
This evolution is a divine law.

Love the Lord and be free. He is the One
Who appears as many, enveloping
The cosmos, without beginning or end.
None but the pure in heart can realize him.

May Lord Shiva, creator, destroyer,
The abode of all beauty and wisdom,
Free us from the cycle of birth and death.

The Fruit of the Tree

No longer am I
The man I used to be;
For I have plucked the fruit
Of this precious tree of life.

As the river flows down the hills
And becomes one with the sea,
So has this weaver's love flowed
To become one with the Lord of Love.

Go deeper and deeper in meditation
To reach the seabed of consciousness.
Through the blessing of my teacher
I have passed beyond the land of death.

Says Kabir: Listen to me, friends,
And cast away all your doubts.
Make your faith unshakable in the Lord,
And pass beyond the land of death.

The Lamp of Wisdom

To all who long and strive to realize the Self,
Illumination comes to them in this very life.
This divine awareness never leaves them,
And they work unceasingly for the good of all.
When the lamp of wisdom is lit within,
Their face shines, whether life brings weal or woe.
Even in deep sleep they are aware of the Self,
For their mind is freed from all conditioning.
Inwardly they are pure like the cloudless sky,
But they act as if they too were like us all.
Free from self-will, with detached intellect,
They are aware of the Self even with their hands at work.
Neither afraid of the world, nor making the world afraid,
They are free from greed, anger, and fear.

When the waves of self-will subside
Into the sea of peace that is the Self,
The mind becomes still, the heart pure,
And illumination comes to us in this very life.
When this supreme state is attained,
They neither rise nor fall, change nor die.
Words cannot describe the supreme state
For it is fuller than fullness can be.

The Brahmin

Cross the river bravely,
Conquer all your passions,
Go beyond the world of fragments,
And know the deathless ground of life.

Cross the river bravely,
Conquer all your passions,
Go beyond your likes and dislikes
And all fetters will fall away.

Who is a true brahmin?
Him I call a brahmin
Who has neither likes nor dislikes,
And is free from the chains of fear.

Who is a true brahmin?
Him I call a brahmin
Who has trained his mind to be still
And reached the supreme goal of life.

The sun shines in the day;
In the night, the moon;
The warrior shines in battle;
In meditation, the brahmin.
But day and night the Buddha shines
In radiance of love for all.

Him I call a brahmin
Who has shed all evil.
He is called *samana,* "the serene,"
And *pabbajita,* "a pure one."

Him I call a brahmin
Who is never angry,
Never causes harm to others
Even when he is harmed by them.

Him I call a brahmin
Who clings not to pleasure.
Do not cause sorrow to others:
No more sorrow will come to you.

Him I call a brahmin
Who does not hurt others
With unkind acts, words, or thoughts.
His body and mind obey him.

Him I call a brahmin
Who walks in the footsteps
Of the Buddha. Light your torch too
From the fire of his sacrifice.

Not matted hair nor birth
Makes a man a brahmin,
But the truth and love for all life
With which his heart is full.

Of what use is matted hair?
Of what use a skin of deer
On which to sit in meditation,
If your mind is seething with lust?

Saffron robe, outward show,
Does not make a brahmin,
But training of the mind and senses
Through practice of meditation.

Not riches nor high caste
Makes a man a brahmin.
Free yourself from selfish desires
And you will become a brahmin.

He has thrown off his chains;
He trembles not in fear.
No selfish bonds can ensnare him,
No impure thought pollute his mind.

Him I call a brahmin
Who fears not jail nor death.
He has the power of love
No army can defeat.

Him I call a brahmin
Who clings not to pleasure,
Like water on a lotus leaf,
Or mustard seed on a needle.

Him I call a brahmin
Ever true, ever kind.
He never asks what life can give,
But "What can I give life?"

Him I call a brahmin
Who has found his heaven,
Free from every selfish desire,
Free from every impurity.
For him no more sorrow will come.
On him no more burden will fall.

———

The Brahmin

Him I call a brahmin
Who has risen above
The duality of this world,
Free from sorrow and free from sin.

He shines like the full moon
With no cloud in the sky.

Him I call a brahmin
Who has crossed the river,
Difficult, dangerous to cross,
And safely reached the other shore.

Wanting nothing at all,
Doubting nothing at all,
Master of his body and mind,
He has gone beyond time and death.

Him I call a brahmin
Who turns his back on himself.
Homeless, he is ever at home;
Egoless, he is ever full.

Him I call a brahmin
Who is free from bondage
To human beings and nature,
The hero who has conquered the world.

Self-will has left his mind;
It will never return.
Sorrow has left his life;
It will never return.

Him I call a brahmin,
Free from I, me, and mine,
Who knows the rise and fall of life.
He will not fall asleep again.

The Brahmin

Him I call a brahmin
Whose way no one can know.
He lives free from past and future;
He lives free from decay and death.

Possessing nothing, desiring nothing
For his own pleasure, his own profit,
He has become a force for good,
Working for the freedom of all.

He has reached the end of the way;
He has crossed the river of life.
All that he had to do is done;
He has become one with all life.

Be Aware of Me Always

SRI KRISHNA:

Those who are free from selfish attachments,
Who have mastered the senses and passions,
Act not, but are acted through by the Lord.
Listen to me now, O son of Kunti,
How one who has become an instrument
In the hands of the Lord attains Brahman,
The supreme consummation of wisdom.

Unerring in discrimination,
Sovereign of the senses and passions,
Free from the clamor of likes and dislikes,
They lead a simple, self-reliant life
Based on meditation, using speech,
Body, and mind to serve the Lord of Love.

Free from self-will, aggressiveness, arrogance,
From the lust to possess people or things,
They are at peace with themselves and others
And enter into the unitive state.

United with the Lord, ever joyful,
Beyond the reach of self-will and sorrow,
They serve me in every living creature
And attain supreme devotion to me.
By loving me they share in my glory
And enter into my boundless being.

All their acts are performed in my service,
And through my grace they win eternal life.

Make every act an offering to me;
Regard me as your only protector.
Make every thought an offering to me;
Meditate on me always.

Drawing upon your deepest resources,
You shall overcome all difficulties
Through my grace. But if you will not heed me
In your self-will, nothing will avail you.

If you say, "I will not fight this battle,"
Your own nature will drive you into it.
If you will not fight the battle of life,
Your own karma will drive you into it.

The Lord dwells in the hearts of all creatures,
And he whirls them round on the wheel of time.
Run to him for refuge with all your strength
And peace profound will be yours through his grace.

I give you these precious words of wisdom;
Reflect on them and then choose what is best.
These are the last words I shall speak to you,
Dear one, for your spiritual fulfillment.

Be aware of me always, adore me,
Make every act an offering to me,
And you shall come to me;
This I promise, for you are dear to me.
Leave all other support, and look to me
For protection. I shall purify you
From the sins of the past. Do not grieve.

Do not share this wisdom with anyone
Who lacks in devotion or self-control,
Lacks the desire to learn, or who scoffs at me.

Those who teach this supreme mystery
Of the Gita to all those who love me
Will come to me without doubt. No one
Can render me more devoted service;
No one on earth can be more dear to me.

Those who meditate on these holy words
Worship me with wisdom and devotion.
Even those who listen to them with faith,
Free from doubts, will find a happier world.

Have you fully understood my message?
Are you free from your doubts and delusions?

ARJUNA:

You have dispelled my doubts and delusions
And made me ready to fight this battle.
My faith is firm now, and I will do your will.

The City of Brahman

In the city of Brahman is a secret dwelling, the lotus
of the heart. Within this dwelling is a space, and within
that space is the fulfillment of our desires. What is within
that space should be longed for and realized.

As great as the infinite space beyond is the space
within the lotus of the heart. Both heaven and earth
are contained in that inner space, both fire and air, sun
and moon, lightning and stars. Whether we know it in
this world or know it not, everything is contained in
that inner space.

Never fear that old age will invade that city; never
fear that this inner treasure of all reality will wither
and decay. This knows no age when the body ages; this
knows no dying when the body dies. This is the real
city of Brahman; this is the Self, free from old age, from
death and grief, hunger and thirst. In the Self all desires
are fulfilled.

The Self desires only what is real, thinks nothing
but what is true. Here people do what they are told,
becoming dependent on their country, or their piece
of land, or the desires of another, so their desires are
not fulfilled and their works come to nothing, both in
this world and in the next.

Those who depart from this world without knowing who they are or what they truly desire have no freedom here or hereafter.

But those who leave here knowing who they are and what they truly desire have freedom everywhere, both in this world and in the next.

Like strangers in an unfamiliar country walking over a hidden treasure, day by day we enter the world of Brahman while in deep sleep but never find it, carried away by what is false.

The Self is hidden in the lotus of the heart. Those who see themselves in all creatures go day by day into the world of Brahman hidden in the heart. Established in peace, they rise above body-consciousness to the supreme light of the Self. Immortal, free from fear, this Self is Brahman, called the True. Beyond the mortal and the immortal, he binds both worlds together. Those who know this live day after day in heaven in this very life.

The Self is a bulwark against the confounding of these worlds and a bridge between them. Day and night cannot cross that bridge, nor old age, nor death, nor grief, nor evil or good deeds. All evils turn back there, unable to cross; evil comes not into this world of Brahman.

One who crosses by this bridge, therefore, if blind, is blind no more; if hurt, ceases to be hurt; if in sorrow, ceases sorrowing. At this boundary night itself becomes day: night comes not into this world of Brahman.

Only those who are pure and self-controlled can find this world of Brahman. That world is theirs alone. In that world, in all the worlds, they live in perfect freedom.

A Garden beyond Paradise

Everything you see has its roots
    in the Unseen world.
The forms may change,
    yet the essence remains the same.

Every wondrous sight will vanish,
Every sweet word will fade.
    But do not be disheartened,
The Source they come from is eternal –
Growing, branching out,
    giving new life and new joy.

Why do you weep? –
That Source is within you,
And this whole world
    is springing up from it.

The Source is full,
Its waters are ever-flowing;
    Do not grieve,
        drink your fill!
Don't think it will ever run dry –
This is the endless Ocean!

From the moment you came into this world
A ladder was placed in front of you
    that you might escape.

From earth you became plant,
From plant you became animal.
Afterwards you became a human being,
Endowed with knowledge, intellect, and faith.

Behold the body, born of dust –
　　how perfect it has become!

Why should you fear its end?
When were you ever made less by dying?

When you pass beyond this human form,
No doubt you will become an angel
And soar through the heavens!

But don't stop there.
Even heavenly bodies grow old.

Pass again from the heavenly realm
　　and plunge into the vast ocean of Consciousness.
Let the drop of water that is you
　　become a hundred mighty seas.

But do not think that the drop alone
Becomes the Ocean –
　　the Ocean, too, becomes the drop!

MAHATMA GANDHI

Self-Surrender

Our existence as embodied beings is purely momentary; what are a hundred years in eternity? But if we shatter the chains of egotism, and melt into the ocean of humanity, we share its dignity. To feel that we are something is to set up a barrier between God and ourselves; to cease feeling that we are something is to become one with God. A drop in the ocean partakes of the greatness of its parent, although it is unconscious of it. But it is dried up as soon as it enters upon an existence independent of the ocean. . . .

As soon as we become one with the ocean in the shape of God, there is no more rest for us, nor indeed do we need rest any longer. Our very sleep is action. For we sleep with the thought of God in our hearts. This restlessness constitutes true rest. This never-ceasing agitation holds the key to peace ineffable. This supreme state of total surrender is difficult to describe, but not beyond the bounds of human experience. It has been attained by many dedicated souls, and may be attained by ourselves as well.

〜

The City of God

Grieve Not is the name of my town.
Pain and fear cannot enter there,
Free from possessions, free from life's taxes,
Free from fear of disease and death.

After much wandering I am come back home
Where turns not the wheel of time and change,
And my Emperor rules, without a second or third,
In Abadan, filled with love and wisdom.

The citizens are rich in the wealth of the heart,
And they live ever free in the City of God.
Listen to Ravidas, just a cobbler:
"All who live here are my true friends."

The Bridge to Immortality

The learned say life is self-created;
Others say life evolved from time. In truth,
The Lord brought the cosmos out of himself.

He is pure consciousness, omnipresent,
Omnipotent, omniscient, creator
Of time and master of the three gunas.
Evolution takes place at his command.

Those who act without thought of personal
Profit and lead a well-disciplined life
Discover in course of time the divine
Principle that all forms of life are one.
They work in the service of the Lord and
Are freed from the law of karma.

Know him to be the primal source of life
Whose glory permeates the universe,
Who is beyond time and space, yet can be
Seen in our hearts in meditation.

Know him to be beyond the tree of life,
Whose power makes all the planets revolve,
Who is both law and mercy, yet can be
Seen in our hearts in meditation.

Know him to be the supreme Lord of lords,
King of kings, God of gods, ruler of all,
Without action or organs of action,
Whose power is seen in myriad ways.

Know him to be the Cause without a cause,
Without a second, parent or master.
May he, Lord of Love, who hides himself in
His creatures as a spider in its web,
Grant us illumination.

The Lord is hidden in the heart of all
Creatures. He watches our work from within
As eternal witness, pure consciousness,
Beyond the reach of the gunas.

The Lord is the operator. We are
But his innumerable instruments.
May we realize him in our consciousness,
The bliss he alone can give us.

Changeless amidst the changing, consciousness
Of the conscious, he grants all our prayers.
May we realize him in our consciousness,
The freedom he alone can give us.

Neither sun nor moon nor star nor fire shines;
Everything reflects the light of the Lord.
May we realize him in our consciousness;
There is no other way to conquer death.

He is the maker of the universe,
Self-existent, omniscient, destroyer
Of death, the source and inmost Self of all,
Ruler of the cycle of birth and death.
May we realize him in our consciousness;
There is no other way to conquer death.

The Bridge to Immortality

He is the protector of the cosmos,
All glory, all-knowing, omnipresent;
How could there be any ruler but he?
May we realize him in our consciousness;
There is no other way to conquer death.

Lord Shiva is my refuge, he who grants
Freedom from the cycle of birth and death.
Lord Shiva is my refuge, he who gave
The sacred scriptures at the dawn of time.
Lord Shiva is my refuge, he who is
The source of purity and perfection.
Lord Shiva is my refuge, he who is
The bridge from death to immortality.
Lord Shiva is my refuge, he whose grace
Has made me long for his lotus feet.

How can we roll up the sky like a piece
Of deerskin? How can we end our misery
Without realizing the Lord of Love who
Is enshrined in our heart of hearts?

If you have deep love for the Lord of Love
And your teacher, the light of this teaching
Will shine in your heart. It will shine indeed!

Setu Prayer

Dear Lord, please fill my heart
with love and devotion for you
and burn out all seeds of selfish desire
and sense craving in my mind.

Grant that I may be carried by you
from this life to the next without suffering
and be born in a holy family
with my heart overflowing
with love and devotion for you
from earliest childhood onwards.

ॐ

E K N A T H   E A S W A R A N

The Message of the Scriptures

Every morning my spiritual teacher, my grandmother, used to go to our ancestral temple to worship the Lord as Shiva. On her return she would place behind my ear a flower she had offered to the Lord in worship and bless me with these simple words: "May you be like Markandeya!"

Markandeya is an illumined teenager in the Hindu scriptures, whose parents prayed for a son who would be completely devoted to Lord Shiva. Their prayer was finally granted – but with the sad condition that their son would die on his sixteenth birthday.

The first word Markandeya lisped as a baby was "Shiva, Shiva." His love for the Lord grew from day to day until it filled his consciousness. When he attained his sixteenth birthday, he learned from his heartbroken parents that Yama, the King of Death, would be claiming him as his victim that day. On hearing this, Markandeya sat down in deep meditation at the feet of Lord Shiva, who is known in Sanskrit as *Mrityunjaya*, the Conqueror of Death.

At the appointed hour, Yama appeared for his victim. But as he was about to carry him away, Lord Shiva arose in the depths of Markandeya's meditation to protect his young devotee. The Lord placed one hand on Markandeya's head in infinite love, and with the other he pointed his trident at the King of Death, who trembled like a leaf in the wind at the sight of Mrityunjaya.

"Don't you know," asked the Conqueror of Death, "that anyone who takes refuge at my feet has gone beyond your power? Markandeya has now become immortal through my grace."

It took years for me to understand that Markandeya's story is not poetry, fantasy, or philosophy. It is possible for every human being to go beyond the reach of death, not in some afterlife but here and now. And not only is it possible, it is our birthright.

This realization lies at the heart of mysticism everywhere. The instruction in the Bhagavad Gita and the Upanishads is clear, complete, and practical. You are neither body nor mind, both of which are subject to change. The body is your external instrument; the mind is your internal instrument. But you are the operator, the *Atman* or Self. This Self is immutable, immortal, indivisible, infinite, the same in every creature. To realize the Self is to attain the supreme goal of life.

This is the purpose of meditation. Self-realization is beyond the senses and the intellect. It comes through a higher mode of knowing, developed through the sincere, systematic, sustained practice of meditation over many years. When the senses are stilled, when the mind is stilled, you are enabled through the infinite love of the Lord to become united with him in the supreme state of *samadhi*. To attain samadhi is to pass beyond death, to realize that you are immortal.

This deathless state of Self-realization can be attained by you while you are living right here on the face of this earth. As the medieval mystic Kabir puts it:

> O friend, know him and be one with him whilst you live.
> If you know him not in life, how can you in death?
> Don't dream that your soul will be united with him
> Because the body-house is demolished by death.
> If he is realized now, he is realized then too;
> If not, you go but to live in the Land of Death.

Lord Shiva is represented traditionally as the Divine Beggar, who comes with his begging bowl to your door for alms. When you offer this beggar food, clothes, money, he refuses to accept them.

"What do you want from me, then?" you ask.

"Your ego," comes the answer: "your selfishness, your separateness. Throw that in my bowl and become united with me, Mrityunjaya, Conqueror of Death."

The scriptures describe Lord Shiva as seated in *sahasrara*, the thousand-petalled lotus, which may well be a spiritual symbol for the millions of cells that make up the human brain. In deep meditation there are many remarkable experiences that make you aware of this thousand-petalled lotus blooming in all its glory. In the stupendous climax of samadhi, you are enabled to wake up from the dream of being just a separate petal into the realization that you are the whole lotus, with the Lord of Love enshrined within it.

This is the message of every major scripture. It is the testimony of mystics everywhere, East or West. So I would like to offer this little anthology with the same blessing I received from my grandmother, which still reverberates through my life: *Meditate. Realize the Self. Transcend death here and now. Become like Markandeya!*

An Eight Point Program

When I came to this country as an exchange professor in 1959, I was invited to speak to many groups of people on the source of India's ancient civilization. At the end of every talk a few thoughtful men and women would come up and ask me, "How can we bring these changeless values into our own daily life?"

"You don't have to change your religion," I assured them, "to do what I have done. The method of meditation I learned is universal. It can be practiced within the mainstream of any religious tradition, and outside all of them as well."

I began by teaching simply what I myself had been practicing for over a decade, illustrating from the scriptures and mystics of the world's great religions. Very quickly this became systematized into eight points, the first and most important of which is meditation. The next few pages are a short introduction to this eight-point program for spiritual growth, which is discussed fully in my book *Meditation*.

1. MEDITATION

The heart of this program is meditation: half an hour every morning, as early as is convenient. Do not increase this period; if you want to meditate more, have half an hour in the evening also, preferably at the very end of the day.

Set aside a room in your home to be used only for meditation and spiritual reading. After a while that room will become associated with meditation in your mind, so that simply entering it will have a calming effect. If you cannot spare a room, have a particular corner. Whichever you choose, keep your meditation place clean, well ventilated, and reasonably austere.

Sit in a straight-backed chair or on the floor and gently close your eyes. If you sit on the floor, you may need to support your back lightly against a wall. You should be comfortable enough to forget your body, but not so comfortable that you become drowsy.

Whatever position you choose, be sure to keep your head, neck, and spinal column erect in a straight line. As concentration deepens, the nervous system relaxes and you may begin to fall asleep. It is important to resist this tendency right from the beginning by drawing yourself up and away from your back support until the wave of sleep has passed.

Once you have closed your eyes, begin to go *slowly*, in your mind, through one of the passages from the scriptures or the great mystics which I recommend for use in meditation. I usually suggest learning first the Prayer of Saint Francis of Assisi (see page 109).

In memorizing the prayer, it may be helpful to remind yourself that you are not addressing some extraterrestrial being outside you. The kingdom of heaven is within us, and the Lord is enshrined in the depths of our own consciousness. In this prayer we are calling deep into ourselves, appealing to the spark of the divine that is our real nature.

While you are meditating, do not follow any association of ideas or try to think about the passage. If you are giving your attention to each word, the meaning cannot help sinking in. When distractions come, do not resist them, but give more attention to the words of the passage. If your mind strays from the passage entirely, bring it back gently to the beginning and start again.

When you reach the end of the passage, you may use it again as necessary to complete your period of meditation until you have memorized others. It is helpful to have a wide variety of passages for meditation, drawn from the world's major traditions. Each passage should be positive and practical, drawn from a major scripture or from a mystic of the highest stature.

The secret of meditation is simple: we become what we meditate on. When you use the Prayer of Saint Francis every day in meditation, you are driving the words deep into your consciousness. Eventually they become an integral part of your personality, which means they will find constant expression in what you do, what you say, and what you think.

2. REPETITION OF THE MANTRAM

A *mantram*, or Holy Name, is a powerful spiritual formula which has the capacity to transform consciousness when it is repeated silently in the mind. There is nothing magical about this. It is simply a matter of practice, as you can verify for yourself.

Every religious tradition has a mantram, often more than one. For Christians, the name of Jesus itself is a powerful mantram. Almost as old is the Jesus Prayer: "Lord, Jesus Christ, son of God, have mercy on us." Catholics also use *Hail Mary* or *Ave Maria*. Jews may use *Barukh attah Adonai*, "Blessed art thou, O Lord," or the Hasidic formula *Ribono shel olam*, "Lord of the universe." Muslims repeat the name of Allah or *Allahu akbar*, "God is great, or *Bismillah ir-Rahman ir-Rahim*, "In the name of God, the Merciful, the Compassionate." Probably the oldest Buddhist mantram is *Om mani padme hum*, referring to the "jewel in the lotus of the heart." In Japan, Buddhists repeat *Namo Amida Butsu*, "I bow to the Buddha of Infinite Light." In Hinduism, among many choices, I recommend *Rama, Rama, Rama*, which was Mahatma Gandhi's mantram.

Select a mantram that appeals to you deeply. In many traditions it is customary to take the mantram used by your spiritual teacher. Then, once you have chosen, do not change your mantram. Otherwise you will be like a person digging shallow holes in many places; you will never go deep enough to find water.

Repeat your mantram silently whenever you get the chance: while walking, while waiting, while you are doing mechanical chores like washing dishes, and especially when you are falling asleep. You will find for yourself that this is not mindless repetition. The mantram will help to keep you relaxed and alert during the day, and when you can fall asleep in it, it will go on working for you throughout the night as well.

Whenever you are angry or afraid, nervous or worried or resentful, repeat the mantram until the agitation subsides. The mantram works to steady the mind, and all these emotions are power running against you which the mantram can harness and put to work.

3. SLOWING DOWN

Hurry makes for tension, insecurity, inefficiency, and superficial living. I believe that it also makes for illness: among other things, "hurry sickness" is a major component of the Type A behavior pattern, which research has linked to heart disease. To guard against hurrying through the day, start the day early and simplify your life so that you do not try to fill your time with more than you can do. When you find yourself beginning to speed up, repeat your mantram to help you slow down.

It is important here not to confuse slowness with sloth, which breeds carelessness, procrastination, and general inefficiency. In slowing down we should attend meticulously to details, giving our very best even to the smallest undertaking.

4. ONE-POINTED ATTENTION

Doing more than one thing at a time divides attention and fragments consciousness. When we read and eat at the same time, for example, part of our mind is on what we are reading and part on what we are eating; we are not getting the most from either activity. Similarly, when talking with someone, give that person your full attention. These are little things, but all together they help to unify consciousness and deepen concentration.

Everything we do should be worthy of our full attention. When the mind is one-pointed it will be secure, free from tension, and capable of the concentration that is the mark of genius in any field.

5. TRAINING THE SENSES

In the food we eat, the books and magazines we read, the movies we see, all of us are subject to the conditioning of rigid likes and dislikes. To free ourselves from this conditioning, we need to learn to change our likes and dislikes freely when it is in the best interests of those around us or ourselves. We should choose what we eat by what our body needs, for example, rather than by what the taste buds demand. Similarly, the mind eats too, through the senses. In this age of mass media, we need to be particularly discriminating in what we read and what we go to see for entertainment, for we become in part what our senses take in.

6. PUTTING OTHERS FIRST

Dwelling on ourselves builds a wall between ourselves and others. Those who keep thinking about *their* needs, *their* wants, *their* plans, *their* ideas cannot help becoming lonely and insecure. The simple but effective technique I recommend is to learn to put other people first – beginning within the circle of your family and friends, where there is already a basis of love on which to build. When husband and wife try to put each other first, for example, they are not only moving closer to each other. They are also removing the barriers of their ego-prison, which deepens their relationships with everyone else as well.

7. READING IN WORLD MYSTICISM

We are so surrounded today by a low concept of what the human being is that it is essential to give ourselves a higher image. For this reason I recommend devoting half an hour or so each day to reading the scriptures and the writings of the great mystics of all religions. Just before bedtime, after evening meditation, is a particularly good time, because the thoughts you fall asleep in will be with you throughout the night.

There is a helpful distinction between works of inspiration and works of spiritual instruction. Inspiration may be drawn from every tradition or religion. Instructions in meditation and other spiritual disciplines, however, can differ from and even seem to contradict each other. For this reason, it is wise to confine instructional reading to the works of one teacher or path. Choose your teacher carefully. A good teacher lives what he or she teaches, and it is the student's responsibility to exercise sound judgment. Then, once you have chosen, give your teacher your full loyalty.

8. SPIRITUAL ASSOCIATION

The Sanskrit word for this is *satsang,* "association with those who are spiritually oriented." When we are trying to change our life, we need the support of others with the same goal. If you have friends who are meditating along the lines suggested here, it is a great help to meditate together regularly. Share your times of entertainment too; relaxation is an important part of spiritual living.

This eightfold program, if it is followed sincerely and systematically, begins to transform personality almost immediately, leading to profoundly beneficial changes which spread to those around us.

How to Use This Book

This book has been designed to be a daily companion, a guidebook for a journey of spiritual transformation. As a collection of mystical statements chosen for the practice of meditation, it naturally would be found where people sit down to meditate – and thousands of earnest men and women have used these passages in meditation. However, the same criteria that make the selections ideally suited for meditation also open up a wealth of applications. The passages have been taught to children, read aloud to the dying, and turned to for renewal and comfort in the press of daily life. Thus this book is intended not only for meditation corners but also for bedside tables and coffee tables, backpacks and briefcases, classrooms and clinics as well as chapels, sanatoriums as well as sanctuaries.

The passages offer in a poetically distilled form the truths of what has been called the "perennial philosophy" – a term put forward by Leibnitz as *philosophia perennis* in the seventeenth century and popularized by Aldous Huxley in his 1945 book of that title. In Hinduism for thousands of years it has been called *sanatana dharma*, "the eternal law," which states that within every creature is a spark of the unchanging Reality underlying existence and that by entering deep within ourselves we can discover that Reality directly.

THE POWER OF THE WORD

When we read these inspired words, reflect on them, write them out, memorize them, meditate on them with profound concentration, they have the capacity to sink into our consciousness, alive with the charge of mystical awareness that first drew them forth. From earliest times, the power of the transcendent word has been recognized as a source of creative potency. Scriptural writings proclaim the origins of the world itself in the resonant fecundity of the word of God.

"In the beginning was the Word, and the Word was with God, and the Word was God," declares Saint John in the familiar opening lines of his New Testament Gospel.

Nearly identical phrasing can be found in the Rig Veda, most ancient of the Hindu scriptures, rooted in an oral tradition many centuries older than Saint John: "In the beginning was Prajapati [God the Creator], with whom was the Word. The Word was verily the supreme Brahman [God the Transcendent]."

The Qur'an, sacred text of Islam, declares: "He it is who has created the heavens and the earth with truth, and on the day He says: 'Be,' it is."

In the lives of the great mystics we get tantalizing glimpses of the creative power of inspired words to bring forth new ways of perceiving the world.

Twenty-five hundred years ago in India, when the Compassionate Buddha delivered his first discourse, the sermon known as "Setting in Motion the Wheel of the Dharma," it not only transformed some skeptical former companions but was the first of thousands of teachings meticulously preserved and practiced to this day.

Saint Anthony, it is said, heard the words of Jesus from the Gospel of Matthew being read aloud: "If thou wilt be perfect, go, sell all that thou hast and give it to the poor and come, follow me; you will have a treasure in heaven." Though he had heard the passage many times before, on this occasion it entered his heart like an arrow of fire. He sold his considerable property and distributed the proceeds. A bit later, another Gospel text, "Take no thought for the morrow," moved him so deeply that he retreated to the Egyptian desert to devote himself to contemplation. He is considered the founder of Christian monasticism and his teachings continue to be a wellspring of inspiration.

In seventh-century Arabia, the first converts to the new faith of Islam were some of the close associates of Muhammad to whom he repeated the electrifying verses branded into his soul in long nights of solitude on Mount Hira. These companions were won over by the stunning grandeur of the language, which had visibly changed the man they knew. Those who are familiar with the classical Arabic of the Qur'an tell us it defies translation – an instance, in the words of a modern commentator, of "human language crushed by the power of the Divine Word."

In thirteenth-century Italy, Saint Clare made a life-altering choice after hearing Francis of Assisi deliver an impassioned sermon, his face lit up with divine love.

These are dramatic examples of the power of holy utterances to realign the individual personality. For most of us, this realignment may be a gradual process over years, decades, even a lifetime. Yet, according to the perennial philosophy, it is part of our human birthright to be privy in our own souls to the drama of transformation for which the saints of every time and place provide the proof. We can claim our birthright by opening our hearts to the transcendent Word.

The sixth-century pope Gregory the Great has described how scripture can speak to us directly:

"It is God who speaks to us, who never ceases to speak to us in these words. Even though they have been fixed in their phrasing for thousands of years, he who makes us hear them today already had us in mind when he inspired them of old, and he is always present to address himself to us through them, as if they were at this instant pronounced for the first time."

Belief in an Almighty is not a prerequisite for gaining access to the immediacy of mystical wisdom. We can respond to the passages as the promptings of our true Self, the best we can become. What *is* required is attentiveness, persistence, and the desire to move from inspiration to insight to action.

The great spiritual traditions of the world have developed systematic methods for engaging the transforming power of sacred words. Through oratory and psalmody, sermon and song, as well as through the more inward and contemplative practices of reading, reflection, and meditation, the truths of the spirit are renewed in the encounter between the questing heart of a seeker and the infused wisdom of the sublime as preserved in scriptural and mystical texts.

This book is organized to support the practice of passage meditation developed by Eknath Easwaran, a precise and effective modern refinement of ancient techniques of internalizing holy words. But the book also facilitates other beneficial ways of working with the passages. Much can be gained, for instance, simply by browsing through the collection of readings. Like the process of animation in which a series of static drawings comes to life when viewed in rapid succession, reading through these passages from different traditions, times, and points of view can arouse a sense of the animating Reality which pervades all life.

LECTIO DIVINA

This collection of spiritual texts also works well with an exercise known in the Christian tradition as *lectio divina* ("sacred reading"), an ancient practice which is undergoing a revival and entering the mainstream of modern spirituality. Monastic tradition from the early centuries of Christianity put great store in the slow, attentive, contemplative perusal of sacred words for the purpose of drinking in the meaning and applying it to the particular needs of the seeker.

The practice has roots in ancient Israel, where recitation, reading, and study of the Torah was regarded as a special task assigned by God – an assignment which must be renewed continuously, as if the one who reads or hears or recites were standing in person on Mount Sinai to receive the Torah afresh. In Judaism, regular reading of the Torah has been a cornerstone of religious observance for many centuries.

A similar approach has been practiced in other traditions. Hinduism, for example, teaches the disciplines of *shravanam*, focused attentiveness to spiritual instruction, and *mananam*, intense reflection on what was received.

To practice *lectio divina* with this book, sit down in a quiet place where you can concentrate fully. Choose a passage and read it through slowly. Close your eyes and reflect on what you have read. Are there any words or phrases that seem especially significant to you? Read the passage through again. You may proceed a page at a time, a paragraph, or even line by line. If you wish, you might jot down a few notes about how the inspired words affect your life and how you might put them into practice. You can refer to the Notes on page 283 for background, context, and further reading related to the passages. The list of passages for changing negative habits of thinking, beginning on page 277, is a helpful guide in choosing passages for particular personal needs.

LECTIO CONTINUA

When *lectio divina* is practiced frequently in an organized sequence of readings, it becomes *lectio continua,* an ongoing and systematic review of inspired texts. For example, the great Christian classic *The Imitation of Christ* has been a manual of daily study for countless seekers since it was first compiled in fifteenth-century Germany. Saint Thérèse of Lisieux is said to have memorized every word. Swami Vivekananda translated key parts of it into Bengali and carried it tucked into a pocket, along with the Bhagavad Gita, during his historic journey to the United States in 1893 to attend the first World Parliament of Religions.

Another example of *lectio continua* comes from Martin Luther: "For some years now," he said, "I have read through the Bible twice every year. If you picture the Bible to be a mighty tree and every word a little branch, I have shaken every one of the branches because I wanted to know what it was and what it meant." The same could be said of Mahatma Gandhi's approach to the Bhagavad Gita.

Detailing the benefits of systematic spiritual reading, Eknath Easwaran tells us: "I find while listening to the *Gospel of Sri Ramakrishna* even for the eleventh time that there are many truths that sink in deeper. This is the main difference between works of literature and works of mysticism: you can read the mystics over and over again and have the impact at a deeper and deeper level. So please don't be under the impression that just because you have read a mystical work once, you are familiar with it. It has to reach deeper and deeper levels of consciousness, which can be attained only by repetition."

The spiritual passages in this book have been arranged as a lectionary of the perennial philosophy and lend themselves readily to daily reading. Read a page or two at a time. When you come to the end of the book, start again at the beginning. You might find it helpful to keep a journal of your readings, noting the insights they provide and the outcomes of your efforts to move from insight to action.

Some people have found that copying out the passages is a wonderful aid to reflection. Each cycle of reading will yield up fresh meanings as your attempts to grow in love and wisdom bring you closer to the living force packed into each mystical statement.

As the nineteenth-century Benedictine Dom Gueranger put it, "The words of God, of the saints, as we repeat them over and over again and enter more and more deeply into their meaning, have a supreme grace to deliver the soul sweetly from preoccupation with itself in order to charm it and introduce it into the very mystery of God."

Abba Nesteros, a fourth-century desert monastic, also spoke of the process of deepening insight: "We must have the zeal to learn by heart the sacred scriptures in their order and to go over and over them without ceasing in our memory. In the measure in which our spirit is renewed by this study, the scriptures also begin to take on a new face. A more mysterious understanding is given us, whose beauty grows with our progress."

These early monastics who developed the practice of *lectio divina* saw it not so much as a way of reading or reflecting as a way of living. Their ruminations on the Gospels found fulfillment in deeds of love and the imitation of Christ. Through reading, listening to, reflecting on, discussing, contemplating, memorizing, and meditating on the life of Jesus of Nazareth, these seekers made the Gospels into a kind of food that was transmuted into the substance of their thinking. In the words of Saint Isaac of Nineveh in seventh-century Syria: "In no way do [the words of scripture] have the effect of having been [merely] entrusted to our memory, but we bring them to birth in the depth of our heart, as natural feelings which are part of our being."

If we look at the biographies of great mystics, we find that the process of internalizing and bringing to life inspired texts is frequently a significant feature of their life stories. Most mystics are firmly lodged within liturgical traditions that surround them, often from birth, with narratives of the spirit, narratives which are in turn revitalized when fulfilled in the words and deeds of these great men and women of God.

In 1948, to cite an example from our own times, upwards of two million people gathered at the Jumna River near New Delhi when the mortal frame of Mahatma Gandhi was consigned to the cremation fires. It was a self-appointed parliament of all religions and of those with no religion, come together to honor the little brown man who seemed to embody the highest and best of what it means to be human. For hours on end, the sound heard at the center of this vast gathering was a recitation of the Bhagavad Gita in its entirety, in the age-old tradition of Hinduism. It was the perfect tribute to one who had imbibed the spirit of the Gita in childhood, turned to it seriously as a young man, and, during his long spiritual struggle, memorized it, translated it, referred to it constantly for guidance. During the nonviolent movement for Indian independence, the Gita was a fixture of Gandhi's daily prayer meetings, where it would take about a week to do a complete reading of all eighteen chapters.

Gandhi called the Bhagavad Gita his mother. It would be more accurate to say he had become the Gita. He had lived out to the fullest extent the way of love in action it espouses and had transformed himself into a living scripture and a renewed revelation.

The deepest level of engagement with the material offered in this book is through the method of passage meditation developed by Eknath Easwaran out of his own experience and tested in the experience of the thousands of men and women from all over the world whom he taught during his forty years of work in the United States. It is a method designed to bring within the reach of the ordinary person an intensity of spiritual practice traditionally confined to the cloister or limited to the extraordinary capacities of a saint. All that is required to begin with is half an hour a day and a willingness to keep at it day after day.

Passage meditation opens up the full range of humankind's most intimate encounters with the divine over the past five thousand years. It can be seen as a way of harnessing the power of the word over thousands of years of spiritual expression. It offers a methodology for internalizing at the deepest, most transforming levels of the mind either the pure essence of a received tradition or a creative synthesis of the perennial philosophy wherever it has appeared.

Most of us in the modern world do not have the supportive framework of the great liturgical cultures that provide continuous nourishment for the spirit in the form of exalted words and images as ubiquitous and available in the past as modern advertising is in our own times. However, our restless, secular, skeptical era does offer an unparalleled opportunity. We have at our fingertips the legacy of centuries of mystical exploration in countless translations, interpretations, and compilations – new ones are appearing all the time. To make the most of our opportunity we need several things:

* We need a framework for making wise choices, adapted to our personal needs, among the flood of materials available.

* We need a systematic way to make our choices viable, building within ourselves the continuous nourishment of spirit that fuels personal growth.

* Most of all, we need a way to draw the power of the word down into the crucible of consciousness in an intricate alchemy

How to Use This Book

of infused wisdom and fresh insight that transforms us from the inside out.

Passage meditation offers all this through daily, silent, utterly focused concentration on memorized selections from the highest mystical expressions of what the human being can be.

This method of meditation naturally requires a preliminary period of working with the passages – choosing the ones you wish to use and then memorizing them by whatever technique works best for you. It is worth noting here that memory is a mental muscle which gets stronger with use. Research suggests that the human brain possesses a remarkable plasticity which can support our efforts to extend our capacities.

Some people are auditory learners and benefit most from reading passages out loud. This process is repeated until a passage can be spoken from memory in preparation for silent repetition during meditation. You might try getting together with other auditory learners for recitation sessions, cuing one another and sharing favorite selections.

Visual learners seem to do better with silently reading sections of a passage over and over until the words are memorized. An alternative is to write out verses by hand. You might keep a small notebook for this purpose and carry it with you to take advantage of odds and ends of time throughout the day.

Use both auditory and visual methods if you find both helpful. Don't be intimidated by long passages. You can break them up into smaller segments and work on them in sequence until the whole passage is mastered. Persistence is crucial. Just when it seems you are getting nowhere you might be delighted to find that an entire sequence of lines will "click in."

To maintain the freshness of your meditation practice, it is important to keep learning new passages. The exercises associated with *lectio divina* and *lectio continua* can be very beneficial in helping you cultivate a repertoire of inspirational passages extending beyond what you might be able to memorize and use in meditation at any one time, greatly enriching your practice.

The selections from world mysticism in this book provide

material for serious and sustained practice of meditation over a lifetime. While the core assertions of these passages hew close to the basic tenets of the perennial philosophy, there is a variety of form and expression to suit different temperaments, traditions, and stages on the spiritual journey. The selections are divided into three parts, very loosely organized to inspire a journey of discovery.

Part 1, "At the Source," features invocations to the springs of our being in the divine ground of existence. "From out of Brahman floweth all that is," declare the ancient Hindu sages who gave us the Upanishads. Says the Chinese mystic Lao Tzu: "The Universe had a beginning, called the Mother of All Things. Once you have found the Mother, you can know her children."

Mystics from diverse traditions marvel at discovering the originating principle of the universe within themselves. "Though the inner chamber of the heart be small," says the Sufi mystic Shabestari, "the Lord of both worlds gladly makes his home there." Saint Symeon the New Theologian exclaims, "All of life wells up in me. He is in my heart, He is in heaven; both here and there He reveals himself to me in equal glory."

Part 2, "Deep Currents," highlights songs of unified desire in which the soul's deepest longings come together in a rush of selfless love. It opens with scriptural injunctions on the way of love, a path which, as Sri Krishna promises in the Bhagavad Gita, "leads sure and swift to me." Where the Torah commands, "You shall love the Lord with all your heart and with all your soul and with all your might," the Buddha counsels, "Let your love flow outward to the universe, a limitless love without hatred or enmity," and Jesus issues a radical challenge: "Love your enemies; bless those that curse you; do good to those that hate you."

These exhortations are followed by a series of ardent songs from the world's great lovers of God, addressed to the object of their longing. "O my Joy and my Desire and my Refuge," sings the Sufi saint Rabi'a of Basra, "my Friend and my Sustainer and my Goal."

Part 2 also includes prayers centered on the transmuted love called compassion or charity, as when Saint Paul tells us "Love is patient and kind; love is not jealous or boastful; it is not arrogant or rude." Also found here are hymns describing the joy of union with the divine, such as this from Kabir: "I am immersed in that great bliss which transcends all pleasure and pain."

Part 3, "Joining the Sea," addresses the end of our journey, where the individual self merges in the measureless sea of Reality called God. "May the river of my life flow into the sea of love that is the Lord," says a hymn from the Rig Veda. "I am the resurrection and the life," we read in the Gospel of John; "whosoever liveth and believeth in me shall never die." In the Chandogya Upanishad we find the triumphant statement: "This is the Self, free from old age, from death and grief, hunger and thirst. In the Self all desires are fulfilled."

Also in this section are prayers of comfort: Saint Francis de Sales advising, "Do not look with fear to the changes and chances of this life"; Mahatma Gandhi sharing the fruits of personal experience: "I can see that in the midst of death life persists, in the midst of untruth truth persists, in the midst of darkness light persists."

From different traditions come statements of those who have fulfilled the purpose of life, who see the eternal at all times. Saint Catherine of Genoa says quietly, "The soul is in such peace and tranquility that it seems to her that both soul and body are immersed in a sea of the profoundest peace." The Buddha states with calm finality, "He has reached the end of the way; he has crossed the river of life. All that he had to do is done. He has become one with all life."

CONCLUSION

There is no higher conception of the human being than that which has been proclaimed in the perennial philosophy down the ages and exemplified in the lives of the great mystics. This book is dedicated to that highest ideal and offers systematic ways for you to make it your own. We hope you will begin by browsing and then stay on for the thrilling journey of discovery

How to Use This Book

down the river of inspiration – the River of Who We Really Are – which flows through these selections of mystical literature all the way to the ocean of God, where life is one and death has no dominion.

In the spirit of the ancient Chinese proverb which says that a journey of a thousand miles begins with just one step, we invite you to put your toe in the water. Or, to express the invitation more directly, in the words heard by Saint Augustine in the garden at Milan which launched him on his own journey of transformation, *Tolle, lege*: "Pick it up and read!"

Using Inspirational Passages to Change Negative Thinking

"Drive out negative thoughts with positive ones," the Buddha advised – anger with compassion, hostility with good will, hatred with love. Daily meditation along the lines recommended in this book (see p. 259) can gradually replace even deep-seated habits of negative thinking with positive ones. The following passages are particularly effective in transforming major negative ways of thinking.

ANGER, HOSTILITY, RESENTMENT, ILL WILL

Sutta Nipata, "Discourse on Good Will" (p. 104)
Narsinha Mehta, "The Real Lovers of God" (p. 148)
Sri Sarada Devi, "The Whole World Is Your Own" (p. 147)
Saint Teresa of Avila, "Her Heart Is Full of Joy" (p. 173)
Gospel of Saint Matthew, "The Sermon on the Mount" (p. 106)
Seng Ts'an, "Believing in Mind" (p. 58)
Lao Tzu, "The Best" (p. 141)
Thomas à Kempis, "Four Things That Bring Much Inward Peace" (p. 199)
Saint Paul, "Epistle on Love" (p. 140)
Saint Teresa of Avila, "Let Nothing Upset You" (p. 206)
Ortha nan Gaidhael, "Silence" (p. 150)
Hazrat Inayat Khan, "Khatum" (p. 97)
Shankara, "Soul of My Soul" (p. 209)
Swami Sivananda, "The Way to Peace" (p. 144)

"UNFINISHED BUSINESS," DISLOYALTY, PROCRASTINATION

Brother Lawrence, "The Practice of the Presence of God" (p. 152)

Tukaram, "The One Thing Needed" (p. 208)

Dhammapada, "The Blessing of a Well-Trained Mind" (p. 183)

Bahya ibn Pakuda, "Duties of the Heart" (p. 154)

Saint Teresa of Avila, "You Are Christ's Hands" (p. 156)

Bhagavad Gita, "Whatever You Do" (p. 166)

Saint Francis de Sales, "I Am Thine, Lord" (p. 122)

Elizabeth of the Trinity, "O My God, Trinity Whom I Adore" (p. 115)

Jewish Liturgy, "Evening Prayer for the Sabbath" (p. 128)

FEAR, ANXIETY, INADEQUACY

Upanishads, "Invocations" (pp. 29, 101, 177)

Rig Veda, "United in Heart" (p. 102) and "God Makes the Rivers to Flow" (p. 178)

Solomon ibn Gabirol, "Adon Olam" (p. 185)

Katha Upanishad, "The Razor's Edge" (p. 80)

Mahatma Gandhi, "The Path" (p. 202)

Bhagavad Gita, "Be Aware of Me Always" (p. 241)

Thomas à Kempis, "Lord That Giveth Strength" (p. 196)

Meera, "The Path to Your Dwelling" (p. 116)

Chandogya Upanishad, "The City of Brahman" (p. 244)

Sutta Nipata, "The Island" (p. 200)

Bhagavad Gita, "What Is Real Never Ceases" (p. 189)

Psalm 23, "The Lord Is My Shepherd" (p. 201)

Chief Yellow Lark, "Let Me Walk in Beauty" (p. 188)

Book of Common Prayer, "I Am the Resurrection and the Life" (p. 179)

Saint Francis de Sales, "Do Not Look with Fear" (p. 207)

Jalaluddin Rumi, "A Garden beyond Paradise" (p. 246)

Psalm 139, "Lord, Thou Hast Searched Me" (p. 52)

Isha Upanishad, "The Inner Ruler" (p. 31)
Amritabindu Upanishad, "The Nectar of Immortality" (p. 84)
Songs of Sri Ramakrishna (pp. 69, 113, 114, 222, 231)
Bhagavad Gita, "The Illumined Man" (p. 74)
Kabir, "Simple Union" (p. 170)
Ansari of Herat, "Invocations" (p. 131)
Saint Teresa of Avila, "Her Heart Is Full of Joy" (p. 173)
Solomon ibn Gabirol, "Adon Olam" (p. 185)
Narsinha Mehta, "The Real Lovers of God" (p. 148)
Thomas à Kempis, "The Wonderful Effect of Divine Love"
     (p. 124)
Tukaram, "Think on His Name" (p. 218)
Dov Baer, "You Must Forget Yourself in Prayer" (p. 61)
Solomon ibn Gabirol, "The Living God" (p. 67)

JEALOUSY

Saint Paul, "Epistle on Love" (p. 140)
Shvetashvatara Upanishad, "The Lord of Life" (p. 90)
Isha Upanishad, "The Inner Ruler" (p. 31)
Saint Patrick, "Christ Be with Me" (p. 149)
Meera, "Life of My Life" (p. 118)
Lao Tzu, "The Best" (p. 141)
Thomas à Kempis, "Lord That Giveth Strength" (p. 196)
Saint Ignatius of Loyola, "Just Because You Are My God"
     (p. 129)
Saint Anselm, "Teach Me" (p. 54)
Bhagavad Gita, "Whatever You Do" (p. 166)
Bahya ibn Pakuda, "Duties of the Heart" (p. 154)
Ansari of Herat, "Invocations" (p. 131)
Bhagavad Gita, "The Way of Love" (p. 110)
Meera, "Singing Your Name" (p. 217)

Saint Francis of Assisi, "The Prayer of Saint Francis" (p. 109)
Thomas à Kempis, "Four Things That Bring Much Inward Peace"
    (p. 199)
Shankara, "Soul of My Soul" (p. 209)
Gospel of Saint Matthew, "The Sermon on the Mount" (p. 106)
Lao Tzu, "Finding Unity" (p. 145)
Rig Veda, "United in Heart" (p. 102)
Dhammapada, "Twin Verses" (p. 86)
Sutta Nipata, "Discourse on Good Will" (p. 104)
Sri Sarada Devi, "The Whole World Is Your Own" (p. 147)
Brother Lawrence, "The Practice of the Presence of God"
    (p. 152)
Psalm 100, "Worship the Lord in Gladness" (p. 30)
Bhagavad Gita, "Whatever You Do" (p. 166)
Tukaram, "The One Thing Needed" (p. 208)
Saint Teresa of Avila, "You Are Christ's Hands" (p. 156)
Mahatma Gandhi, "The Path" (p. 202)
Mahatma Gandhi, "In the Midst of Darkness" (p. 203)
Psalm 23, "The Lord Is My Shepherd" (p. 201)
Bhagavad Gita, "The Illumined Man" (p. 74)
Fakhruddin Araqi, "The Shining Essence" (p. 50)
Isaiah, "When You Call" (p. 146)
Mishkat al-Masabih, "I Come to Him Running" (p. 181)
Swami Ramdas, "Such Is a Saint!" (p. 94)

Saint Francis of Assisi, "The Prayer of Saint Francis" (p. 109)
Bhagavad Gita, "The Illumined Man" (p. 74)
Bhagavad Gita, "The Way of Love" (p. 110)
Ansari of Herat, "Invocations" (p. 131)
Dhammapada, "Twin Verses" (p. 86)
Dhammapada, "The Brahmin" (p. 236)
Thomas à Kempis, "The Wonderful Effect of Divine Love"
    (p. 124)
Psalm 23, "The Lord Is My Shepherd" (p. 201)
Chandogya Upanishad, "The City of Brahman" (p. 244)
Eknath Easwaran, "Setu Prayer" (p. 253)
Swami Sivananda, "Universal Prayer" (p. 55)
Shankara, "Soul of My Soul" (p. 209)

Notes

Arranged in alphabetical order by author or scripture. SMALL CAPITALS indicate related references within these notes. Sources of the texts are given here when known, with formal acknowledgments on pages 323–324. For unfamiliar words here or in the passages themselves, see the glossary on page 321.

AMRITABINDU UPANISHAD
"The Nectar of Immortality," p. 84
The Amritabindu ("drop of the nectar of immortality") is one of several UPANISHADS titled with the Sanskrit word *bindu*, "droplet," indicating succinctness. Translated by Eknath Easwaran in *The Upanishads* (Nilgiri Press, 1987).

ANSARI OF HERAT
"Invocations," p. 131
Abdullah al-Ansari (1006–1088) was a Persian poet and mystic in the Sufi tradition of Islam. A beloved figure in Herat, now in Afghanistan, his shrine is a place of pilgrimage for Sufis and other admirers from all over the world. He wrote in Dari, a Persian language closely akin to Farsi and one of the main languages of modern Afghanistan, where his writings are considered a literary and spiritual treasure. His works are part of the expansion of the Islamic ideal as it merged into the mainstream of a wide range of cultures and languages. The essence of Sufism is the search for direct experience of God as the divine Beloved. The verses collected here are selected from *The Persian Mystics: Invocations of al-Ansari al-Harawi,* tr. Sardar Sir Jogendra Singh (J. Murray, 1939).

ANSELM, SAINT
"Teach Me," p. 54

Saint Anselm (1033–1109) was a defining figure of medieval Christianity. Originally from northern Italy, he entered monastic life in Normandy and was soon elected an abbot despite his desire to remain a contemplative. One biographer notes a touching scene: Anselm prostrating himself before the assembled monks, begging them not to burden him with office; the monks in turn prostrating themselves, begging him to accept. He was later sent to England as Archbishop of Canterbury, a post he also tried to avoid (the bishop's staff had literally to be forced into his hand) but filled with dignity and effectiveness. In the midst of heavy administrative duties and the complex politics of the era, he found time to write philosophical treatises in defense of his faith which remain a touchstone of Christian theology. This passage captures the devotional strain in his personality, appealing directly to the heart and needing no argument. The translation is from David A. Fleming, s.m., ed., *The Fire and the Cloud* (Paulist Press, 1978).

ARAQI, FAKHRUDDIN
"The Shining Essence," p. 50

Fakhruddin Araqi (1213–1289) was an important poet and mystic of the golden age of Sufism, whose life story gives a glimpse of the cosmopolitan breadth of thirteenth-century Islamic civilization. Born in Persia, he was a child prodigy destined for a life of scholarship. But when he was a young man the course of his life was altered by a band of spiritual wanderers who awakened the dormant spiritual yearning in his heart. He joined them, making his way to India where he spent twenty-five years in the Punjab with a Sufi master. After the death of his teacher in 1266, Araqi traveled west to Oman, Mecca, and Damascus, eventually reaching Konya in what is now Turkey. He became a noted exponent of the Spanish Sufi philosopher and mystic Ibn al-'Arabi. In states of spiritual exaltation, Araqi composed perfectly constructed verses as commentaries on Arabi's doctrines regarding the primacy of love as the source of knowledge. He is buried in Damascus, where Arabi's tomb is also located and where visitors traditionally honor both, saying of Arabi, "This was the ocean of the Arabs," and of Araqi, "This was the ocean of the Persians." This passage from the *Lama'at* ("Divine Flashes") is from Jonathan Star, *The Inner Treasure* (Putnam/Tarcher, 1999).

AUGUSTINE, SAINT
"Entering into Joy," p. 230

Augustine of Hippo (354–430), one of the founders of the Western Christian tradition, was born in North Africa and achieved success as a teacher and rhetorician in Rome and Milan. After being drawn to Christ he became Bishop of Hippo in North Africa, where he lived into the last stages of collapse of the Roman Empire – the city was besieged as he lay dying. His writings played a formative role in the emergence of medieval Christendom. His *Confessions*, a masterpiece of autobiographical literature, is the story of a brilliant and passionate man who learned to channel all his aspirations toward God. This passage from book 9, chapter 10, is part of the description of an episode of union with God experienced jointly by Augustine and his mother, Saint Monica. Translated for this book by Michael N. Nagler.

AZIKRI, RABBI ELEAZAR
"Beloved of the Soul," p. 123

Eleazar ben Moses Azikri (1533–1600) was a scholar, poet, ascetic, and student of the Kabbalah, the mystical tradition of Judaism which focuses on the relationship between the transcendent, unknowable Godhead and the dynamic expression of God's being in creation. He lived in Safed in upper Galilee, where he and a few friends formed a pact to dedicate themselves entirely to study of the scriptures and the worship of God. (It is said he spent two-thirds of his time writing and one-third in silent contemplation.) His major work, *Sefer Haredim*, is a spiritual manual that contains much practical wisdom, such as this comment: "The commandment 'Love your neighbor as yourself' includes the observance of the entire Torah. On the other hand, hatred includes the violation of the entire Torah." The prayer "Beloved of the Soul" (*Yedid Nefesh*) was written for his friends. Published the year after he died, it was so popular among Jewish communities all over the Mediterranean that it became part of the Sabbath liturgy. This translation is by Rabbi Harvey Spivak.

BABA KUHI OF SHIRAZ
"Only God I Saw," p. 77

Baba Kuhi (d.1050) was an Islamic mystic and Sufi master whose tomb on a mountainside in Shiraz, Iran, has been a place of pilgrimage since the eleventh century. Legends say anyone able to stay awake by the shrine for forty nights will receive the blessing of immortality, the gift of poetry, and the fulfillment of one's heart's desire. In the fourteenth century, the renowned mystic and poet Hafiz accepted the challenge out of hopeless love for a beautiful woman. By the end of the fortieth night of his vigil, he found that his heart's desire had been transmuted to longing for a vision of God – a vision that was finally granted to him after forty years of seeking. Baba Kuhi's prayer expresses the fulfillment of ardent spiritual yearning. The translation is from Reynold A. Nicholson, *The Mystics of Islam* (G. Bell & Sons, 1914).

BAHYA IBN PAKUDA, RABBI
"Duties of the Heart," p. 154

Bahya ibn Pakuda, an obscure judge of the rabbinical court in Saragasso, left an enduring legacy as a Jewish moral philosopher. His treatise on the essence of the Mosaic law (*Hovot ha-Levarot* or "Duties of the Heart," from which this passage comes), written in Muslim Spain in the eleventh century, provides proof of the beauty and power that can result when different cultures meet in the heart of a man or woman of God. It was modeled on similar works of Muslim mystics and was meant to counterbalance the emphasis on ritual and ethical observances in the Jewish community. The original was written in Arabic and translated into Hebrew by Judah ibn Tibbon in the late twelfth century. This translation is by Rabbi Harvey Spivak.

BERNARD OF CLAIRVAUX, SAINT

"That Wondrous Star," p. 204

Bernard of Clairvaux (1090–1153) is known today for his Biblical commentaries, which light up the mystical depths of scripture, and for his devotion to Mary. As founder of the abbey of Clairvaux in France, Bernard was a leader of the Cistercian reform which aimed at returning the Benedictines to the original purity of the Rule of Saint Benedict. A charismatic personality and a powerful force in the ecclesiastical and secular movements of his times, he drew hundreds to the monastic life and counseled thousands more, including popes and kings. Toward the end of his life, he rose from his sickbed to travel through the Rhineland preaching against a wave of anti-Semitic persecutions; he is remembered as a "righteous Gentile" by Rhineland Jews, many of whom bear his name. His path was one of contemplation fulfilled in action, which he compared to a reservoir overflowing with love that spills out into the lives of others. This passage from his *Homilies in Praise of the Blessed Virgin Mary* (Hom. 2:17) invokes an ancient image of Mary as *stella maris* or "star of the sea," interpreted as rescuer of those floundering in the turbulence of worldly life.

BHAGAVAD GITA

"The Illumined Man," p. 74
"The Way of Love," p. 110
"Whatever You Do," p. 166
"All Paths Lead to Me," p. 182
"What Is Real Never Ceases," p. 189
"The Eternal Godhead," p. 210
"Be Aware of Me Always," p. 241

The Bhagavad Gita ("Song of the Lord") is Hinduism's best-known scripture and one of India's greatest gifts to the world, a masterpiece of world poetry on which countless mystics have drawn for daily practical guidance. Composed sometime between the fifth and second centuries B.C.E., it has the character of an Upanishad, inserted into the epic *Mahabharata* just before the outset of a devastating dynastic war. Against this background the teaching of the Gita unfolds, couched as a dialogue between Sri Krishna, a divine incarnation, and his friend and disciple Arjuna, a warrior prince who represents anyone trying to live a spiritual life in the midst of worldly activity and conflict. Part of Mahatma Gandhi's genius was to interpret the Gita's teachings as a manual for selfless action in a world of conflict, where the battle that forms its background is essentially the "war within": the struggle between selfishness and selflessness in the depths of human consciousness.

"What Is Real Never Ceases" (Gita 2:13–30) marks the beginning of Krishna's instruction to Arjuna, who has withdrawn in despair just before the outbreak of the fratricidal conflict that is the climax of the dramatic action of the *Mahabharata*. These verses represent the transition from the epic narrative to the Upanishadic dialogue of spiritual instruction. Here Krishna exhorts the despairing Arjuna not to be deluded by surface appearances but to fix his mind on what is unchanging and deathless. The eighteen verses which conclude this chapter, "The Illumined Man" (Gita 2:54–72), were considered by Gandhi to contain the essence of the Gita's teaching. "All Paths Lead to Me" is from Gita 4:9–11; "The Eternal Godhead," dealing with the time of death, is from Gita 8:5–22. "Whatever You Do" is the close of chapter 9; "The Way of Love" is the whole of chapter 12.

"Be Aware of Me Always" (Gita 18:49–73) comes from the very end of this scripture: having taken Arjuna to the root of his being, Krishna now sends him forth full of resolve to act in the world with awareness of the divine unity of life. These passages, translated for meditation by Eknath Easwaran, are in his *Bhagavad Gita* (Nilgiri Press, 1985) and *The Bhagavad Gita for Daily Living* (3 vols: Nilgiri Press, 1975, 1979, 1984).

THE BOOK OF COMMON PRAYER
"I Am the Resurrection and the Life," p. 179
The Book of Common Prayer was created in 1529 to serve the needs of the Church of England in place of the Latin liturgies it had abandoned. It has since gone through many editions for other times and churches, but all versions retain the lofty confidence that makes the first edition, attributed to Thomas Cranmer, a masterpiece of

English literature. This passage, from the readings for the Order for the Burial of the Dead, is a soaring declaration of certainty in the face of bodily death.

CATHERINE OF GENOA, SAINT
"A Sea of Peace," p. 226

The Christian saint Caterina Fieschi Adorno (1447–1510) was born to a noble family in Genoa, Italy, where she spent all of her life. For many years after an obligatory marriage to a nobleman at the age of sixteen she was caught between spiritual yearnings and the demands of her position in society. At twenty-seven she experienced a soul-shattering conversion which created within her a permanent condition of union with God. Her life became an outpouring of active love combining intense devotion and practical service of the sick and destitute. Transformed by her example, her husband joined her in her work in the hospital of Genoa, where after his death she continued to labor tirelessly. She confided to those who gathered around her a little about her extraordinary inner states, but much more has been captured in her books (such as *Dialogues of Soul and Body*). This translation is from G. Ripley, tr., *Life and Doctrine of Saint Catherine of Genoa* (n.p., 1874).

CHAITANYA, SRI
"O Name, Stream Down in Moonlight," p. 220

Sri Chaitanya (c. 1485–1533), a Hindu mystic of Bengal, India, taught a path of devotion to God in the form of Krishna through continuous chanting of his name. Chaitanya's way of love was open to all, regardless of sect, caste, or social status. He is regarded as an originator of *kirtan,* a form of devotional singing from which the "Songs of Sri RAMAKRISHNA" in this book have been selected.

THE CHANDI
"Hymn to the Divine Mother," p. 36

In the Hindu tradition the creative power of the Godhead is worshiped under many names and forms as the Divine Mother. This hymn is from the Chandi or Devi Mahatmya, a Sanskrit scripture which glorifies the Divine Mother as protector of her devotees and vanquisher of the negative forces in consciousness. This translation is from Swami Prabhavananda and Christopher Isherwood, *Prayers and Meditations Compiled from the Scriptures of India* (Vedanta Press, 1967).

CHANDOGYA UPANISHAD
"This Is the Self," p. 49
"You Are That," p. 224
"The City of Brahman," p. 244

The Chandogya is one of the most ancient of the UPANISHADS, a vast chorus (*chandogya* means "singer") of many parts and sections. "You Are That" shows a dramatic style characteristic of the Upanishads, in which wisdom is transmitted in scenes of arresting tenderness. The context of the teaching in this passage is as familiar now as it was thousands of years ago: a son returns from school proud of his learning. Here, the father probes to see if the boy has gained spiritual wisdom as well as intellectual knowledge and proceeds to fill in what conventional learning failed to teach. The famous refrain "You Are That" (Sanskrit *Tat tvam asi*) is one of the four *mahavakyas* or "great utterances" that encapsulate the teachings of the Upanishads: the Self, the divine essence in every creature, and Brahman, the eternal Godhead, are one and the same. These selections, translated for meditation by Eknath Easwaran, are in his *Upanishads* (Nilgiri Press, 1987).

CLARE, OF ASSISI, SAINT
"The Mirror of Eternity," p. 93

A fascinating persuasiveness of personality informs the story of Chiara Offreduccio (1194–1253), noblewoman of Assisi, Italy, known to history as Saint Clare. Just as her family had eventually to yield to her decision to leave a luxurious life and join Saint FRANCIS OF ASSISI and his small following of mendicants, a succession of popes had eventually to yield to her insistence that the sisters of the Franciscan experiment would maintain its traditions in a pure form. It is said that even her cat obeyed her, bringing her needed items when she was too ill to get up – a miracle by modern as well as medieval standards. The Rule for her Poor Ladies, approved shortly before her death (she died holding on to a copy) formalized for posterity the way of joyful simplicity which Francis had begun. Evelyn Underhill, in her classic book *Mysticism,* calls Clare "the hidden spring of Franciscan spirituality." This passage comes from one of her letters (Ltr. 3:12–16) to Saint Agnes of Prague.

DHAMMAPADA
"*The Saint," p. 78*
"*Twin Verses," p. 86*
"*Give Up Anger," p. 142*
"*The Blessing of a Well-Trained Mind," p. 183*
"*The Brahmin," p. 236*

The Dhammapada is an ancient collection of the Buddha's teachings in verse form which has become part of the spiritual heritage of humanity. *Buddha* – literally "one who is awake" – is the title given to prince Siddhartha Gautama (c. 563–483 B.C.E.) after he attained illumination. The pampered and sheltered prince had renounced his kingdom, a small principality in the foothills of the Himalayas, to learn how to overcome disease, decay, and death. His story is one of the paradigmatic narratives of transformation in the annals of world mysticism, a template of the human spirit. The heart of his message is captured in the Dhammapada, part of the Sutta Pitaka of the Buddhist canon of scripture. Like the BHAGAVAD GITA and the *Imitation of Christ,* the Dhammapada can best be understood as a guidebook for living in accordance with the highest goals of the spiritual life. It consists of teachings arranged thematically by early – perhaps even direct – disciples who wanted a ready compilation of the Buddha's teaching.

"Twin Verses," the opening chapter, gives the core of the Buddha's presentation of the spiritual life as the training of the mind. Mara the Tempter (the name may come from the Sanskrit *mri,* "to die") personifies death and the attachments that bind one to a separate, self-centered existence; "saffron robe" refers to the monastic apparel of the Buddha and his followers. "The Brahmin," the concluding chapter of the Dhammapada, reveals the Buddha's emphasis on mental states rather than physical appearance. The word *brahmin* refers to a member of the priestly caste; the Buddha maintains that the true brahmin is not someone who belongs to a particular social position or shows outward insignia of spirituality like the matted hair of the ascetic or the saffron robe of the monk, but one who has attained stillness of mind. These selections were translated for meditation by Eknath Easwaran. *See also* SUTTA NIPATA.

DOV BAER OF MEZHIRECH
"You Must Forget Yourself in Prayer," p. 61
Dov Baer (d. 1772), *magid* (itinerate preacher) of Mezhirech, was the chief disciple and successor of Rabbi Israel ben Eliezer, the Baal Shem Tov or "Master of the Good Name," founder of the Hasidic movement of Jewish mysticism, which places devotional prayer at the center of the spiritual life. Dov Baer was a distinguished scholar when he went to the simple, saintly Baal Shem for some medical advice. He stayed on for the rest of his life when he realized his learning was the outer shell of religion while the Baal Shem Tov possessed the soul of it. Dov Baer formalized and popularized the Hasidic teachings of the search for union with God in all things. This passage invokes basic concepts of the Kabbalah, the ancient tradition of Jewish mysticism; "World of Thought" in this passage refers to the highest of ten levels of reality, a state in which individual awareness remains undifferentiated from the divine. Dov Baer wrote no books, but many of his students published his teachings; this passage comes from the best known of these collections, *Magid Devarav le-Ya'akov,* first published in 1781. The translation is by Arthur Green and Barry W. Holtz, from their book *Your Word Is Fire: The Hasidic Masters on Contemplative Prayer* (Jewish Lights, 1993).

ECKHART, MEISTER
"One with God," p. 79
Eckhart von Hochheim (c. 1260–1327), regarded by many as the father of German mysticism, shines far beyond the confines of a particular tradition. Born in Thuringia, he entered the Dominican order at age fifteen and rose quickly in its ranks, teaching in Paris,

Strasbourg, and Cologne and holding a series of administrative posts. His sermons on the nature of the unknowable Godhead were thrilling to many but incomprehensible or threatening to others. As one listener put it, "The Master speaks to us about Nothingness. If a man does not understand that, the Light Divine has never shone in him." Eckhart died with a charge of heresy pending and some points of his writing were condemned posthumously, but his works and teachings were kept alive by distinguished disciples like Heinrich Suso and Johannes Tauler and by the seventeenth-century mystic known as Angelus Silesius. Eckhart was rediscovered in the nineteenth century and today is honored as one of the purest exponents of the perennial philosophy. This selection is from chapter 6 of his earliest book, *Talks of Instruction,* written for his novices when Eckhart was in his thirties.

EKNATH EASWARAN
"Setu Prayer," p. 253

Eknath Easwaran (1910–1999), founder of the Blue Mountain Center of Meditation and its director throughout his lifetime, developed the method of meditation on inspirational passages that is the basis for this book. The Setu Prayer (*setu* is Sanskrit for "bridge") was one of his daily personal prayers during the last years of his life. It embodies the ideal of his Setu Program, which is based on truths held in all major religions: that death is not the end of life but only the closing of one chapter, and that what comes next is shaped by how we think and live now.

ELIZABETH OF THE TRINITY
"O My God, Trinity Whom I Adore," p. 115

Less well known than her older contemporary THÉRÈSE OF LISIEUX, Blessed Elizabeth of the Trinity (1880–1906) resembles Thérèse in the uncompromising intensity of her interior life of prayer. Unlike the shy Thérèse's sheltered childhood, however, Elizabeth's early life in a French army captain's family was one of travel, parties, and friends, which the vivacious and beautiful young woman, a gifted pianist, enjoyed thoroughly. Nonetheless, under the surface a riptide of spirituality grew stronger until, at age nineteen, it swept her into the silent precincts of the Carmelite convent in Dijon, where she spent the rest of her brief life. By the time of her death at twenty-six, after a painful struggle with Addison's disease, she had won through to the still, pure center of being – for her expressed as the Holy Trinity. This translation is from *Elizabeth of the Trinity: The Complete Works, Volume One,* tr. Sister Aletheia Kane, o.c.d. (ICS Publications, 1984).

FRANCIS DE SALES, SAINT
"I Am Thine, Lord," p. 122
"Do Not Look with Fear," p. 207

This French Catholic saint (1567–1622), a Bishop of Geneva, was noted for his sermons to ordinary people urging the pursuit of sanctity amid worldly responsibilities. "Wherever we are," he said, "we may and ought to aspire to the perfect life." His two major works, *Introduction to the Devout Life* and *Treatise on the Love of God,* are compilations of his advice to parishioners and remain treasured guidebooks. A period of profound despair in his early years – which he overcame through prayer – deepened an already compassionate outlook. "Francis's great work was to show how ordinary life can be sanctified," notes one modern commentator. "Sweetness and graciousness are his key words . . . they represent a reconciliation of the outward beauty and the tough inner core of the Christian life." "Do Not Look with Fear" is a widely popular distillation of a chapter in the *Introduction.* "I Am Thine, Lord," equally well known, comes from the *Treatise on the Love of God;* this version follows the translation of Miles Car, 1630.

FRANCIS OF ASSISI, SAINT
"The Prayer of Saint Francis," p. 109

Francis Bernardone (c. 1181–1226), perhaps the most universally loved of Christian saints, was born in Assisi, Italy. At age twenty-two, after a sudden illness that brought him almost to the point of death, he left his home and inheritance to follow an injunction that he felt he received from Christ himself: "Francis, rebuild my Church." With the eagerness that was a hallmark of his personality, he set about repairing a tiny broken-down chapel on the outskirts of Assisi, begging for stones and singing while he worked. His directness, humility, and uncontainable joy drew others. Within a few years, three great Franciscan orders grew around the monks, nuns, and lay disciples who responded to his example of universal love and selfless service, following the way of Jesus as set forth in the Gospels. By the time of his death there were brown-robed Franciscans walking the roads of Europe and the lands bordering the Mediterranean. Saint CLARE OF ASSISI and others consolidated the movement that remains vital eight hundred years later, and many recent biographies testify to the influence of this joyful mystic who now belongs to the whole world. It is not known when the prayer associated with his name first appeared in writing, but James Meyer, O.F.M., notes in *The Words of St. Francis* (Franciscan Herald Press, 1952) that "a passage which strongly recalls the Peace Prayer" is found in the *Sayings of Brother Giles,* and that Giles, one of Francis's earliest disciples, was a fervent imitator and "very like him in native and inspired wisdom." Whatever the written source, Francis's spirit is faithfully captured in this widely cherished prayer.

GABIROL, SOLOMON IBN. *See* IBN GABIROL, SOLOMON

GANDHI, MAHATMA
"The Path," p. 202
"In the Midst of Darkness," p. 203
"Self-Surrender," p. 248

Mohandas K. Gandhi (1869–1948; *Mahatma* means "great soul") was born in British India and led his country to freedom through a thirty-year struggle based completely on nonviolence. His formulation of *satyagraha* ("holding to truth") as a systematic method for transforming conflict into unity among individuals, communities, and nations, is one of the inspired innovations of the twentieth century. His daily guidebook was the BHAGAVAD GITA, a core scripture of Hinduism, which he translated into his life. When he fell to an assassin's bullet in January 1948, Albert Einstein was among the millions around the world who mourned, saying, "Generations to come, it may be, will scarce believe that such a one as this ever in flesh and blood walked upon the earth." Gandhi's own estimation of himself was characteristically different: "I have not the slightest doubt that any man or woman can achieve what I have, if he or she would make the same effort and cultivate the same hope and faith."

"The Path" and "In the Midst of Darkness," from articles Gandhi wrote for his weekly paper *Young India* in the 1920s, are included in many collections of Gandhi's writings, including *My Religion* (Ahmedabad, India: Navajivan, 1955). Gandhi read "In the Midst of Darkness" for the Columbia Gramophone Company while he was in England working for India's independence in 1931 – the first and last time his voice was preserved in a studio recording. "Self-Surrender" is an excerpt from a letter published in *From Yeravda Mandir: Ashram Observances* (Navajivan, 1945) *Mandir* means "temple"; Yeravda was the prison where Gandhi spent much time during the Indian struggle for independence, reading widely and writing voluminously in his nonstop conversation with the world.

THE GOSPEL OF SAINT MATTHEW
"The Sermon on the Mount," p. 106
These verses (Matt. 5:3–16, 43–48; 6:9–13) have been called the essence of Jesus' teachings. It has been said that if the rest of the New Testament were lost, it would be possible to retain the radical purity of the Christian ideal through these words alone. Saint AUGUSTINE called the Sermon on the Mount "a perfect standard of the Christian life." As a portrait of the perfected person, the Sermon on the Mount finds its truest legacy in the long succession of mystics whose common creed is the imitation of Christ. This translation is from the King James Version (1611).

HASAN KAIMI BABA
"The Path of Love," p. 158
Hasan Kaimi (d. 1691) was a seventeenth-century Sufi poet from Bosnia. This poem is still loved and recited by the people of Sarajevo.

HAZRAT INAYAT KHAN. *See* INAYAT KHAN

HILDEGARD OF BINGEN
"In Your Midst," p. 165
Hildegard of Bingen (1098–1179) was a Benedictine abbess and mystic of medieval Germany. After entering religious life at age eight and receiving a rudimentary education, she lived quietly, confiding her visions to one or two close companions. Then, at forty-two, she experienced an overpowering revelation which illumined the meaning of spiritual texts and enjoined her to record and explain her inner experience. Inspired works of theology, poetry, musical composition, painting, natural science, and public service flowed from her from then on. In a rare personal comment, she described the light she experienced continuously within: "From my infancy up to the present time, I now being more than seventy years of age, I have always seen this light, in my spirit and not with external eyes, and I name it 'the cloud of the living light.' But sometimes I behold within this light another light which I name 'the living light itself.' And when I look upon it, every sadness and pain vanishes from my memory, so that I am again as a simple maid and not as an old woman." This translation, by Mary Ford-Grabowsky, is from her collection *Prayers for All People* (Doubleday, 1995).

IBN GABIROL, SOLOMON
"The Living God," p. 67
"Adon Olam," p. 185
A Spanish poet, philosopher, and mystic of the Jewish tradition, Solomon ibn Gabirol (c. 1021–1058) wrote hundreds of poems in Biblical Hebrew which have become an important part of the Judaic heritage. His philosophy, written in Arabic, drew upon the diverse traditions – classical, Jewish, Christian, and Islamic – of eleventh-century Muslim Spain. His writings on the relation between God as the First Cause and the world as an emanation of God exerted much influence upon later Jewish mystics and Christian theologians. *Adon Olam* ("Lord of the Universe"), translated for this book by Ellen

Lehmann Beeler, is, after the Psalms, perhaps the most popular hymn in the Jewish liturgy. "The Living God" is from *The Jewel in the Lotus,* ed. Raghavan Iyer (Concord Grove Press, 1983).

IGNATIUS OF LOYOLA, SAINT
"Just Because You Are My God," p. 129

Ignatius Loyola (1491–1556), founder of the Society of Jesus (known commonly as Jesuits) of the Roman Catholic Church, began life as a courtier and soldier during the reign of Ferdinand and Isabella of Spain, concerned chiefly with his career and the pleasures of a well-placed young man. After being wounded by a cannonball during a battle with the French in 1521, he spent a wrenchingly painful convalescence in his ancestral castle at Loyola. To pass the time he requested his favorite reading, the romances of chivalry, which were the pulp fiction of the times. None being found anywhere in the castle, he was brought narratives of the life of Christ and the lives of the saints, which, over the long months of his recovery, gradually gave new shape to his dreams of glory as he immersed himself in stories of self-effacing heroism and love for God. Completely transformed, he turned his martial spirit and tremendous capacity for suffering to a spiritual quest which continues to influence the world. His renowned *Spiritual Exercises,* widely followed today, capture the methodology of an inner convalescence in which he struggled to discern the divine will and to live it out no matter the cost.

INAYAT KHAN, HAZRAT
"Prayer for the Peace of the World," p. 96
"Khatum," p. 97
"Prayer for Peace," p. 139

Hazrat Inayat Khan (1882–1927), founder of the Sufi Order International, was born in north India into a distinguished Muslim family of musicians noted for their universality of outlook. He became a gifted *vina* player who toured all over India. In Hyderabad he met a Sufi teacher who altered the course of his life, guiding him to a high degree of spiritual awareness. His teacher's dying words launched him on a new mission: "Fare forth into the world, my child, and harmonize the East and the West with the harmony of thy music. Spread the wisdom of Sufism abroad, for to this end art thou gifted by Allah, the most Merciful and Compassionate." In 1910 he sailed for the United States and spent the remaining seventeen years of his life in North America and Europe teaching what he called "that ancient wisdom from the one and only source." Although Sufism is traditionally part of the mystical heritage of Islam, Hazrat Inayat Khan developed a pattern of worship and spiritual practice that draws upon the major religious traditions. "Khatum" (the word means "placing a seal") is recited at the close of the Sufi Order International worship service. These prayers are all from the literature of the Sufi Order International.

ISAIAH
"When You Call," p. 146
The Book of Isaiah, probably the most quoted of the prophets in the Jewish and Christian scriptures, is today considered to be a compilation of inspired utterances of three different prophets over about three hundred years. The third of these – "Third Isaiah" – most likely lived during the sixth century B.C.E., giving messages of exhortation, warning, and hope ("a new heaven and a new earth") to the Jewish people during a time of rebuilding and recovery. Chapter 58 is widely cited for its emphasis on charity and compassion as opposed to ritual observance. These verses (58:9–11) are from the most recent translation done for the Jewish Publication Society, *Tanakh: The Holy Scriptures* (JPS, 1985).

ISHA UPANISHAD
"The Inner Ruler," p. 31
The Isha Upanishad is customarily placed first in Hindu collections of the UPANISHADS as a tribute to the poetic precision with which it conveys the essence of these ancient scriptures. When Mahatma Gandhi was asked if he could put the secret of his life into three words, he quoted from its opening verse: *Tena tyaktena bhunjitah,* "Renounce and enjoy." If all the Indian scriptures were reduced to ashes save for this verse, he said, Hinduism would still endure

forever. The last verses are traditionally recited for one who has died. Translated for meditation by Eknath Easwaran.

JALALUDDIN RUMI
"A Garden beyond Paradise," p. 246

Jalaluddin Rumi (c. 1207–1273), a poet and mystical genius of the Sufi tradition within Islam, has been called "the greatest mystical poet of any age." His father was a well-known scholar in Balkh, a cosmopolitan center of both Islamic and Buddhist learning located near the legendary Silk Road in what is now Afghanistan. In 1219 the family headed west, barely ahead of the armies of Genghis Khan. After years of travel they finally reached Konya (now in Turkey), capital of the Seljuk Empire. In 1244 a wandering Sufi ascetic, Shams of Tabriz, initiated the scholarly Jalaluddin into the highest levels of divine inebriation in God. After a few brief years Shams disappeared, mysteriously and forever, and Jalaluddin was plunged into a grief which drew from him the inspired poetry for which he is known. His masterworks, the *Divan-e Shams-e Tabrizi* ("Works of Shams of Tabriz") and the *Mathnawi* ("rhyming couplets"), transmute the sorrow of human loss into the joy of union with the divine Beloved. "A Garden Beyond Paradise," found in the *Divan,* is from *A Garden Beyond Paradise: The Mystical Poetry of Rumi,* ed. Jonathan Star and Shahram Shiva (Bantam, 1992).

JEWISH LITURGY
"Sabbath Prayer," p. 83
"Evening Prayer for the Sabbath," p. 128
"Mourner's Kaddish," p. 184

"Evening Prayer for the Sabbath" is a selection from Jewish liturgy appearing in *The Union Prayerbook for Reform Judaism.* "Mourner's Kaddish" is a traditional rendering of the Kaddish – an ancient Jewish prayer in Aramaic repeated at every worship service; the word means "sanctification" – recited in memory of the dead. The passage makes no mention of death, instead offering the mourners a chance to express hope for the welfare of all and to affirm the greatness of God even in times of sorrow.

KABIR

"*The Temple of the Lord,*" *p. 40*
"*The Unstruck Bells and Drums,*" *p. 168*
"*The River of Love,*" *p. 169*
"*Simple Union,*" *p. 170*
"*Weaving Your Name,*" *p. 221*
"*The Fruit of the Tree,*" *p. 234*

Kabir was a fifteenth-century mystical poet and saint honored by both Hindus and Muslims. Not much is known of his life, which was spent in a tiny shop on one of the winding alleyways of Varanasi (Benares), north India, where he followed his trade as a weaver. His thousands of songs and couplets in vernacular Hindi express direct experience of the divine, infusing the mysticism of the Upanishads with the Sufi's ecstatic love. Legends say that at Kabir's death, Hindus came to carry his body to the cremation ground and Muslims came to bury him. Yet when the cloth covering the body was lifted, all that could be seen was a heap of flowers, a fitting fulfillment of his song:

> Be your own light;
> Open your eyes and see
> That Rama and Allah are One!

"The Temple of the Lord" is from *The Jewel in the Lotus,* ed. Raghavan Iyer (Concord Grove Press, 1983); "The Unstruck Bells and Drums" is from a translation by Rabindranath Tagore. Other passages are free renderings by Eknath Easwaran.

KATHA UPANISHAD

"*Perennial Joy,*" *p. 62*
"*The Razor's Edge,*" *p. 80*
"*The Immortal,*" *p. 212*
"*The Tree of Eternity,*" *p. 227*

One of the most dramatic of the UPANISHADS, the Katha tells the story of Nachiketa, a daring teenager who goes to Yama, the King of Death, to learn the secret of immortality. In "Perennial Joy" (part 1, canto 2) Yama begins his teaching with the secret of what endures and what is merely fleeting. In "The Tree of Eternity," the conclusion of this Upanishad, Yama completes the teaching and Nachiketa fulfills his quest, attaining immortality. These selections, translated for meditation by Eknath Easwaran, are in his *Upanishads* (Nilgiri, 1987).

KENA UPANISHAD
"That Invisible One," p. 56
Like the SHVETASHVATARA UPANISHAD, the Kena opens with a series of questions on the nature of reality (*kena* means "by whom," the first word of the text). Here, however, the inquiry is not directed outward to the cause of the cosmos but inward to the source of consciousness itself. Yet the conclusion is the same: Kena, "This Self is not someone other than you"; Shvetashvatara, "The Self is hidden in the hearts of all." In the UPANISHADS, all roads lead to the Self, the divine core of consciousness. Translated by Eknath Easwaran in *The Upanishads* (Nilgiri Press, 1987).

KOOK, ABRAHAM ISAAC, RABBI
"Radiant Is the World Soul," p. 39
Abraham Isaac Kook (1865–1935) is considered the foremost of modern Jewish mystics, a man of God who dealt with the practical problems of his people in a turbulent time while striving constantly to infuse their struggle with spiritual purpose. He was once asked how to respond to hatred and gave the penetrating reply that to counteract *sinat hinam*, gratuitous hatred, one must practice *ahavat hinam*, gratuitous love. The translation of this prayer is by Ben Zion Bokser in *Abraham Isaac Kook* (Paulist Press, 1978).

LAO TZU
"Holding to the Constant," p. 34
"Mother of All Things," p. 35
"The Best," p. 141
"Finding Unity," p. 145
Lao Tzu ("Master Lao," c. 604–531 B.C.E.), a legendary sage of ancient China, is considered the founder of Taoism. The legends relate that he worked as an archivist in the royal court until he decided to withdraw completely from worldly activities. As he was leaving the

kingdom forever, a gatekeeper begged him to record his teachings for posterity. He sat down and quickly wrote out a series of poetic statements about how to live in harmony with the natural order of the universe – verses that have been treasured for twenty-five hundred years as the *Tao Te Ching* ("The Way and Its Power"). "The Best" is from chapter 8, "Holding to the Constant" from chapter 16, "Mother of All Things" from chapter 52, and "Finding Unity" from chapter 56. "Ten thousand things" refers to the multiplicity of the phenomenal world, which is contrasted with Tao, "the Way," the ultimate reality. These translations, done for this book by Stephen H. Ruppenthal, are included in his *Path of Direct Awakening: Passages for Meditation* (Berkeley Hills, 2003).

LAW, WILLIAM
"The Deepest Part of Thy Soul," p. 48

An Anglican theologian and writer of eighteenth-century England, William Law (1686–1761) held a position as tutor in the family of the historian Edmond Gibbon before retiring to live quietly and write treatises of profound depth and wide influence. Gibbon said of him, "If Mr. Law finds a spark of piety in a reader's mind he will soon kindle it into a flame." His best-regarded book is *A Serious Call to a Devout and Holy Life,* one of the works which John Wesley, founder of Methodism, credited for crystalizing his "explicit resolve to be all devoted to God." The selection included here is a pure statement of the perennial philosophy from the Protestant tradition.

LAWRENCE, BROTHER
"The Practice of the Presence of God," p. 152

"Brother Lawrence" (Nicholas Herman, c. 1605–1691) lived almost sixty years as an obscure lay brother among the Carmelites in seventeenth-century Paris. From humble origins (a former soldier and footman), he took no formal vows but assisted in the practical work of the community, mainly as a helper in the kitchen. In this hidden role he perfected the practice of remembering God in all things and at all times, attaining a degree of sanctity that drew people to him for counsel. The little collection of letters and conversations known as *The Practice of the Presence of God,* pieced together after his death (less than a week after this letter was written) is an underground classic of Christian devotion.

MECHTHILD OF MAGDEBURG
"Lord, I Bring Thee My Treasure," p. 119

Born into a prosperous and cultured Catholic family, Mechthild (c. 1212 - 1282) left home in her twenties to become a beguine or lay sister in Magdeburg, Germany. She drew on the rich devices of chivalric romance to pour out her love for God in poetry of timeless originality and appeal ("Lord, I cannot dance unless you lead me"). Her poems, scribbled on scraps of paper that were not collected until after her death, were soon being circulated all over Europe. This popular appeal, and the striking resemblances between her imagery and Dante's, suggest the possibility that Mechthild might have been the prototype for Matelde in the *Divine Comedy*, who appears to the poet in an earthly paradise on the other side of Lethe: "a solitary woman moving, singing, and gathering up flower on flower – the flowers that colored all her pathway." This translation is by Lucy Menzies, from *The Revelations of Mechthild of Magdeburg* (Longmans, Green and Co., 1955).

MEERA
"The Path to Your Dwelling," p. 116
"Come, Beloved," p. 117
"Life of My Life," p. 118
"The Power of the Holy Name," p. 215
"Even with Your Last Breath," p. 216
"Singing Your Name," p. 217

Meera (c. 1498–1547), one of the best loved of Hindu mystics, was a princess of the Rajputs, a people of northwestern India known for their fierce courage – a spirit she channeled into her passionate love for God in the form of Krishna. After her husband's death, his family so persecuted her for her devotional practices that she left the palace and wandered on pilgrimage. Wherever she went she joined other devotees in singing and dancing in praise of God. Her songs, passed down by wandering minstrels, are known and sung today throughout India. Widely translated, these poems of love have become part of the treasure-house of world mysticism. These are free renderings for meditation by Eknath Easwaran.

THE MISHKAT AL-MASABIH
"I Come to Him Running," p. 181

The Mishkat al-Masabih is a fourteenth-century collection of *hadith* (sayings and actions of the Prophet Muhammad) compiled by Sheikh Wali al-Din al-Tabrizi (d. 1348). Though not part of the Qur'an, *hadith* have canonical weight within Islam. Recorded by those closest to the Prophet, they have been a source of profound inspiration in Islamic mysticism and popular devotion. This compilation is highly regarded because it traces the traditional source of each saying.

NARSINHA MEHTA
"The Real Lovers of God," p. 148

This is Mahatma Gandhi's favorite hymn from his own Hindu tradition. It was composed in Gujarati by Narsinha Mehta (1414–1480), a saint, poet, and musician whose devotional hymns in the vernacular are still cherished. This is a free rendering for meditation by Eknath Easwaran.

NATIVE AMERICAN TRADITION
"Great Life-Giving Spirit," p. 186

This passage expresses the sense of sacredness and interconnectedness of the natural world which is at the heart of the Native American spiritual tradition. *See also* YELLOW LARK.

NEWMAN, JOHN HENRY, CARDINAL
"Shine through Us," p. 130

There are several versions of this prayer in circulation, varying slightly to accommodate prayer by individuals or by groups, by Catholics or by non-Catholics. This is appropriate, for John Henry Newman (1801–1890) lived fully half of his life as a Protestant, becoming well known as a speaker for the evangelical Oxford movement, before his conversion in 1845, when he went on to become equally well known as Cardinal Newman, defender of the Catholic faith. This version is from Daphne Rae's book on Mother Teresa of Calcutta and the Missionaries of Charity, *Love Until It Hurts* (Harper & Row, 1981), where it appears along with the Prayer of Saint FRANCIS OF ASSISI as one of the daily prayers of this community dedicated to serving the poorest of the poor.

OMKAR, SWAMI
"Prayer for Peace," p. 138
Composed by Swami Omkar (1895–1982), a Hindu mystic and teacher known for his sweetly generous nature, founder of Shanti Ashram in Andhra Pradesh and the Peace Center on the Nilgiris, south India.

THE ORTHA NAN GAIDHEAL
"Silence," p. 150
"This Morning I Pray," p. 151
The tradition of Celtic Christianity, active from the earliest centuries after Christ in Ireland, Scotland, Wales, Britain, and Brittany, retains deep roots in an ancient indigenous spirituality which comes to life in these prayers from the *Ortha nan Gaidheal* or *Carmina Gadelica,* Alexander Carmichael's nineteenth-century collection of Scottish oral literature. The verses convey the sense of sanctity informing every aspect of daily life, a compelling feature of Celtic prayer in general, which includes blessings for each simple act – rising in the morning, lighting a fire, entering or leaving a room, weaving or plowing, lying down at night – as a means of keeping the mind turned toward God. The close link between the diurnal and the eternal is made explicit in a beautiful morning blessing from the same collection:

> O God, who brought me from the rest of last night
> Unto the joyous light of this day,
> Bring me from the new light of this day
> Unto the guiding light of eternity.

PAKUDA, BAHYA IBN. *See* BAHYA IBN PAKUDA

PARAMANANDA, SWAMI
"Source of Our Existence," p. 45
"O Infinite Being! page 46
"Origin of All," p. 47

One of the first Indian teachers to bring ancient Hindu wisdom to the United States, Paramananda (1884–1940) was following in the footsteps of his own teacher, Swami Vivekananda, one of the foremost disciples of Sri RAMAKRISHNA. Paramananda entered the Ramakrishna Order of monks at age seventeen and went on to a life of tireless effort, writing, speaking, traveling the world, and founding spiritual communities based on the principles of his teacher. Four centers, two in the United States (Vedanta Centre and Ananda Ashrama) and two in India, carry on his work.

PATRICK, SAINT
"Christ Be with Me," p. 149

This passage is from a hymn traditionally ascribed to Saint Patrick, who came to Ireland as a Christian missionary early in the fifth century and became its patron saint. Born a citizen of the Roman Empire, he was captured as a young boy and spent several years in slavery in Ireland before obtaining his freedom. He trained in Gaul (France) as a monk and priest and then returned to the land of his captivity. There he spent many years as an itinerant preacher, inspiring thousands and founding churches and monasteries. The prayer from which this passage is taken is known as "The Breastplate of Saint Patrick" because it was composed as a "breastplate of faith" for protection against the enemies of his work.

PAUL, SAINT
"Epistle on Love," p. 140

One of the main founders of the Christian tradition, in his early days Saint Paul was Saul, a Jewish tent-maker in Tarsus (Asia Minor, now Turkey) soon after the time of Jesus. He was a persecutor of the early Christians until he experienced a cataclysmic vision while traveling to Damascus. Later he said of this experience: "I am crucified with Christ: nevertheless I live; yet not I, but Christ liveth in me."

Having absorbed the cultural heritage of the Roman Empire (he was a Roman citizen), the Hellenic civilization of Asia Minor (he spoke Greek), and the pure Judaic tradition (he was educated in Jerusalem), Paul was well placed to bring the message of Christ to a wide audience. His letters of inspiration, exhortation, and guidance to various struggling congregations make up a significant part of the New Testament; this famous passage (1 Corinthians 13, Revised Standard Version) was written to the group in Corinth. Paul traveled and taught throughout Asia Minor and Greece until his death in Rome, around 65 C.E.

PSALMS

"Worship the Lord in Gladness" (Psalm 100), p. 30
"Lord, Thou Hast Searched Me" (Psalm 139), p. 52
"The Earth Is the Lord's" (Psalm 24), p. 89
"The Lord Is My Shepherd" (Psalm 23), p. 201

The Bible's Book of Psalms is a compilation of 150 hymns attributed to several ancient authors over a period of about a thousand years. Since earliest times it has formed a core component of Jewish and Christian liturgy. *Psalm* is a Greek translation of a Hebrew word for "praise," and it is evident that these poems were intended to be sung. Psalms were recited daily in the temple in ancient Jerusalem and they remain integral to the yearly pattern of readings in synagogues as well as churches. Christian monastics have for centuries chanted the Book of Psalms as part of the divine office of daily worship. Taken as a whole, the Psalms comprise an intimate unfolding of the heart to God, covering the spectrum of human emotions.

"Worship the Lord in Gladness" is an exuberant song of praise for the Most High. "Lord, Thou Hast Searched Me" (vv. 1–19, 23–24) reviews in intimately personal terms the powers of the divine – omniscience ("Thou hast known me"), omnipresence ("Whither shall I go from Thy spirit?"), omnipotence ("I am fearfully and wonderfully made") – and concludes with the startling request that He who has fashioned this soul and knows everything about it should search it still more and be part of every thought. "The Earth Is the Lord's" was probably sung in Biblical times as accompaniment to carrying the

Holy of Holies into the tabernacle; as an interiorized expression, it can be read as a welcoming of the Lord into our hearts. "The Lord Is My Shepherd," surely one of the best-loved passages in the Jewish and Christian scriptures, is a statement of faith in the Lord's goodness in all circumstances, couched in imagery that resonates deeply in the Western imagination. These translations were done for the Jewish Publication Society: Psalm 100 is from *Tanakh: The Holy Scriptures* (JPS, 1985); the others are from the 1917 edition, very similar to the King James Bible.

RABI'A
"Night Prayer," p. 120
"Dawn Prayer," p. 121

Rabi'a al-Adawiyya lived from c. 717 to 801 in the city of Basra, now in southern Iraq. She is considered a major saint and founding figure among the Sufis, who credit her with bringing the doctrine of divine love to the center of the Sufi way. Her life embodied the root meaning of the term *islam*: complete surrender to the will of God. Orphaned early and sold into slavery, she was granted freedom, so say the legends, when her master saw her praying late at night, enveloped in a light that filled the house. She then took up the austere life of a desert hermit, continuously immersed in God. Though she sought attention from no one, she was recognized in her lifetime as a teacher of high stature and many visitors made their way to her door. Numerous tales, prayers, and conversations from her life have come down to us through almost thirteen hundred years of Sufi commentators, including her famous outburst: "Lord, if I love you out of fear of hell, cast me into hell; if I love you out of hope of heaven, close its gates to me; but if I love you for the sake of loving you, do not deny yourself to me!" It was her custom to pray throughout the night, sleeping only for a short time before dawn and then arising to begin her morning prayers. This version of "Night Prayer" is from *Muslim Devotions: A Study of Prayer-Manuals in Common Use,* by Constance E. Padwick (SPCK, 1961); "Dawn Prayer" is from *Rabi'a the Mystic & Her Fellow Saints in Islam,* by Margaret Smith (Cambridge, 1928).

RAMAKRISHNA, SRI, SONGS OF

"Dwell, O Mind, within Yourself," p. 69
"Dive Deep, O Mind," p. 113
"I Have Joined My Heart to Thee," p. 114
"Chant the Sweet Name of God," p. 222
"Thou One without a Second," p. 231

Sri Ramakrishna (1836–1886) was born in a small village in Bengal, north India, and lived out his days as a simple priest of the temple to the Divine Mother at Dakshineswar, near Calcutta. Yet he encompassed within his vast inner experience the spiritual practices of various Hindu paths, Islam, and Christianity, convincing himself experientially that all these religions offer disciplines leading to the same realization of God. He considered himself a child of the Divine Mother and lived in continuous awareness of her. In the last years of his life his evident spiritual greatness drew a stream of visitors awed by his exalted states of mind and inspired conversation. Among them were a number of young men mostly from Calcutta's educated and worldly middle class who were transformed by their contact with him and went on to take his message worldwide through the Ramakrishna Order of monks and the Ramakrishna Mission of humanitarian services. One of his householder disciples kept a detailed diary of these years, the work known in English as *The Gospel of Sri Ramakrishna* (Ramakrishna-Vivekananda Center, 1942), a unique record of the daily life and teachings of a God-conscious person. These songs by various composers, selected from the *Gospel,* are among his favorites from the joyful sessions in his little room. See also SARADA DEVI.

RAMDAS, SWAMI

"Divine Mystery," p. 37
"Such Is a Saint!" p. 94
"The Central Truth," p. 95
"Unshakable Faith," p. 157
"He Is Omnipresent," p. 171
"How Great Is His Name!" p. 219

Swami Ramdas (1884–1963) was born Vittal Rao in a devout Hindu home in Kerala, south India. He led an ordinary life as a householder and textile technician until, plagued by episodes of doubt and idleness, he was initiated by his father into the use of a mantram – the repetition with deep devotion of the name of God, whom he called Rama. The practice transformed his life: he became a pilgrim, accepting joyfully and with no little humor whatever befell him. "The Central Truth" is from his book *In the Vision of God* (repr. Blue Dove Press, 1995); the poems are from *Poems*, by Swami Ramdas (Anandashram, India, 1984).

RAVIDAS
"The City of God," p. 249
A Hindu cobbler of fifteenth-century Varanasi (Benares) in north India, Ravidas is remembered for his hymns and his gentle piety, which drew many seeking souls to his shop. Like the poems of his contemporary KABIR, his songs in the Hindi vernacular overcame distinctions of caste and creed. A noted exemplar of the Bhakti movement, which underwent a renaissance in north India at this time, Ravidas is said to have influenced the saint and poet MEERA. "The City of God" is considered one of his most beautiful hymns; this is a free rendering for meditation by Eknath Easwaran.

RIG VEDA
"United in Heart," p. 102
"God Makes the Rivers to Flow," p. 178
The Rig Veda is one of the four Vedas that form the scriptural fountainhead of Hinduism. Each Veda is comprised of four sections of increasingly interior spiritual expression, beginning with hymns for public worship (such as the two examples given here) and concluding with the sublime statements of mystical Reality known as the UPANISHADS – also called Vedanta, "the end of the Vedas." Probably compiled in written form sometime toward the end of the second millennium B.C.E., the Vedas were preserved long before that in a unique oral transmission that continues to this day. Hindu tradition holds the Vedas to be eternal, existing independently of any oral or written expression. "God Makes the Rivers to Flow" is a free rendering by Eknath Easwaran; "United in Heart," translated by Swami

Prabhavananda and Christopher Isherwood, is from their *Prayers and Meditations Compiled from the Scriptures of India* (Vedanta Press, 1967).

RUMI. *See* JALALUDDIN RUMI

SARADA DEVI, SRI
"The Whole World Is Your Own," p. 147
These words are revered as the last message of Sri Sarada Devi (1853–1920), wife and spiritual companion of Sri RAMAKRISHNA, the Hindu mystic and world teacher. Their remarkable partnership was largely hidden during Ramakrishna's lifetime, but after his passing this simple village woman helped Ramakrishna's disciples establish a legacy that continues to flourish, and gave initiation and comfort to thousands who sought her blessing. From *Holy Mother*, by Swami Nikhilananda (Ramakrishna-Vivekananda Center of New York, 1962).

SENG TS'AN
"Believing in Mind," p. 58
Seng Ts'an (d. 606) is honored as the Third Patriarch of Ch'an Buddhism, a doctrine brought to China from India by the First Patriarch, Bodhidharma, early in the sixth century. Ch'an Buddhism focuses on attaining enlightenment through the practice of meditation – *ch'an* comes from the Sanskrit *dhyana*, "meditation," and the term passed into Japanese as *zen*. Tradition says that Seng Ts'an came to the Buddha's path in his forties but quickly reached the highest level and inherited his master's position. For the next fifteen years he wandered throughout the country, exemplifying simplicity and compassion. This passage is excerpted from his *Hsin Hsin Ming* ("Believing in Mind"), which blends Buddhist and Taoist concepts in what is considered one of the earliest and most influential of Zen writings. The "great Way" and the "ten thousand things" are Taoist formulations indicating the eternal order of the universe and the passing phenom-

enal world. Translated for this book by Stephen H. Ruppenthal; a fuller version is included in his *Path of Direct Awakening: Passages for Meditation* (Berkeley Hills, 2003).

SHABESTARI, MAHMUD
"The Mirror of This World," p. 38

Mahmud Shabestari (c. 1250–1320) is known through his only work, the venerated *Gulshan-i Raz* ("Garden of Secrets" or "Secret Rose Garden"), a masterpiece of Sufi literature. Shabestari spent his life in Tabriz, a city in what is now northwestern Iran, during a golden age of Sufi mysticism that included ARAQI and JALALUDDIN RUMI. This translation is from Jonathan Star, *The Inner Treasure* (J. P. Putnam/Tarcher, 1999).

SHANKARA
"Soul of My Soul," p. 209
"Thy Holy Name," p. 223

A seminal figure of the Hindu tradition, Shankara (c. 788–820) was born in Kerala state, south India, and entered monastic life as a teenager. It is said he convinced his mother to allow him to renounce the world only after a crocodile seized his foot while he was swimming. When he cried out to her his wish to surrender his entire being to God at that moment, his distraught mother gave him her blessing. The crocodile, having played its role in history, then released his foot. Shankara's commentaries on the UPANISHADS, the BHAGAVAD GITA, and other key scriptures systematized and revitalized the spiritual heritage of Hinduism, which he presented as *advaita*, "not two": the principle that there is no reality but Brahman, the supreme Godhead. Honored as an exemplar of the path of *jnana*, spiritual wisdom, he is also considered the source of widely cherished devotional hymns such as the two included here. "Soul of My Soul," translated for this book by Brian Ruppenthal, is from a hymn to Shiva; "Thy Holy Name" is a stanza from a hymn in praise of the Divine Mother.

Shantideva

"The Miracle of Illumination," p. 68

Shantideva is revered in the Mahayana tradition of Buddhism. Born a king's son in the eighth century in what is now Gujarat, north India, he renounced his throne to become a monk at the renowned Buddhist center of learning in Nalanda. Tradition relates that at first his fellow monks, perhaps given to over-rigorous austerities, did not think highly of what they felt was his penchant for sleeping and eating too much. They devised a session of reciting the scriptures to test his mettle. When his turn came, he asked if they wanted to hear old sutras or something new. They opted for something new, and Shantideva then recited the whole of his masterwork, the *Bodhicharyavatara,* a verse exploration of the path of the *bodhisattva* – one who, after attaining *nirvana* (illumination), returns to the sphere of human life for the sake of teaching others. He earned not only the respect of his fellows but a permanent place in the roster of Buddhist saints. These verses from the *Bodhicharyavatara* were translated for this book by Stephen H. Ruppenthal; they are included in his *Path of Direct Awakening: Passages for Meditation* (Berkeley Hills, 2003).

The Shvetashvatara Upanishad

"The River of God," p. 42 (Canto 1)
"The Lord of Life," p. 90 (Canto 2)
"Hidden in the Heart," p. 159 (Canto 3)
"The One Appearing as Many," p. 192 (Canto 4)
"Love the Lord and Be Free," p. 232 (Canto 5)
"The Bridge to Immortality," p. 250 (Canto 6)

One of the most beautiful of the Upanishads, the Shvetashvatara is dedicated to Shiva, who represents God as the bestower of immortality. It begins ("The River of God," canto 1) with a series of urgent questions; one can almost picture the students pressing close – the root meaning of the term *upanishad* is "to sit down nearby" – as an illumined teacher reveals the First Cause, the Lord of Love, hidden in the world "as butter is hidden in cream." "The One Appearing as Many" elaborates the concept of *maya,* the hypnotic illusion of separateness which gives rise to suffering and sorrow, here presented as a divine game of hide-and-seek in which the Lord conceals himself in his multifaceted creation. These six selections, the whole of this Upanishad, were translated for meditation by Eknath Easwaran; they are included in *The Upanishads* (Nilgiri Press, 1987).

SIVANANDA, SWAMI
"*Universal Prayer,*" *p. 55*
"*The Way to Peace,*" *p. 144*

Swami Sivananda (1887–1963), one of the influential twentieth-century teachers who helped to bring the universal aspects of the Hindu tradition to a world audience, was born Kuppuswamy Iyer in a village in south India. A brilliant student, he became a physician and spent ten years in Malaysia as a hospital director noted for his sweet personality and selfless service. The gift of a book led to his immersion in the scriptures of several traditions. He gave up his medical practice and returned to India to devote himself to the quest for God, wandering all over the country before settling down in the Himalayas on the banks of the Ganges. The depth of his spiritual attainments drew followers who helped him establish the Divine Life Society in 1936. Since his passing in 1963, his students continue to teach the ideals of love, service, meditation, and the unity of all religions. The "Universal Prayer" is carved into a marble pillar, in Hindi and in English, at the Divine Life Society's world headquarters in Rishikesh, India.

THE SUTTA NIPATA
"*Discourse on Good Will,*" *p. 104*
"*The Island,*" *p. 200*

These passages are from the Sutta Nipata, which (like the DHAMMAPADA) forms part of the Sutta Pitaka, the part of the Theravada Buddhist scriptures which preserves the direct teachings of the Buddha and his main disciples. The written canon, dating from the first century B.C.E., reflects an oral tradition that began during the Buddha's time and was formalized soon after his passing as direct disciples codified his memorized teachings. "Discourse on Good Will" is from Sutta Nipata 1:143–152; "The Island," from Sutta Nipata 5. These translations by Stephen H. Ruppenthal are included in his *Path of Direct Awakening: Passages for Meditation* (Berkeley Hills, 2003).

SYMEON THE NEW THEOLOGIAN, SAINT
"I Know That He Reveals Himself," p. 60

Saint Symeon (949–1022) is one of only three mystics in the Eastern Orthodox tradition of Christianity honored with the title of Theologian, which in this tradition signifies someone who can speak of God on the basis of personal experience. (The others so honored are Saint John the Evangelist and Saint Gregory Nazianzen.) Symeon came from Asia Minor, now Turkey. His teaching that God can be realized in the heart through meditation and prayer aroused opposition that led to his banishment as abbot of the St. Mamas monastery in Constantinople. When finally invited to return, he chose to remain with a small band of followers in a run-down chapel on the eastern shore of the Bosporus, continuing his writings and teachings. He couched his personal experience of God in terms of light, generally referring to himself in the third person: "He saw nothing but light all around him and did not know whether he was standing on the ground ... he was wholly in the presence of immaterial light and seemed to himself to have turned into light." Experiences like these were the source of his confidence in telling others: "Do not say that God cannot be seen by a human being. Do not say that a mere human cannot behold the Divine Light, or that it cannot be seen in the present time." Largely unknown in the West until the twentieth century, Symeon is beginning to gain a wider audience through English translations of major works like the *Discourses* and *Hymns*. "I Know That He Reveals Himself" is from Hymn 13.

TEJOBINDU UPANISHAD
"The Shining Self," p. 70

The Tejobindu ("drop of splendor"), given here in its entirety, is one of a small group of UPANISHADS whose names end in *bindu*, "droplet," because of their conciseness. "The three stages of meditation" here refers to the three stages of classical yoga, *dharana, dhyana,* and the culminating state of *samadhi,* in which the distinction between knower and known disappears. Translated by Eknath Easwaran in *The Upanishads* (Nilgiri Press, 1987).

TERESA OF AVILA, SAINT
"You Are Christ's Hands," p. 156
"I Gave All My Heart," p. 172
"Her Heart Is Full of Joy," p. 173
"Let Nothing Upset You," p. 206

Teresa de Cepeda y Ahumada (1515–1582), born in Avila, Spain, is one of the best-loved saints in the Christian tradition and a mystical genius of universal appeal, who followed both the way of action and the way of contemplation. A lively, talented girl, she entered a Carmelite convent at eighteen, spending twenty years there in spiritual struggle before she was able to dedicate herself completely to God. After she became established in her experience of the continuous presence of Jesus, her life became one of intense practical activity, built around her mission of returning the Carmelite order to the austere purity in which it had been founded. She traveled throughout Spain in rickety ox-carts in every kind of weather, establishing convents, teaching, writing, and meeting with all ranks of society, always centered in the deepest spirituality and inner peace. Her three most important books (in English, the *Autobiography* [*Libro de la Vida*], *The Way of Perfection,* and *The Interior Castle*) are classics of world mysticism, offering in her warm, colloquial style one of the fullest accounts available of the inward life of the spirit. The little poems given here were written without thought of publication. "You Are Christ's Hands" is said to be from a letter written to her nuns; "Let Nothing Upset You," dear to Catholics and non-Catholics around the world, was found in her breviary after her death. Translated for this book by James Wehlage.

THÉRÈSE OF LISIEUX, SAINT
"Living on Love," p. 162

Thérèse Martin (1873–1897) was born into a profoundly devout Catholic family in which all five daughters entered religious life. She was admitted to a Carmelite convent in her hometown of Lisieux

Notes

when she was fifteen and lived an utterly hidden existence there until her death at age twenty-four. These scant biographical details conceal an inner spiritual journey – narrated in her slender autobiography, *The Story of a Soul* – that places her among the great mystical pioneers in any era. Called "the greatest saint of modern times" by Pope Pius X, she is loved around the world for her "little way of spiritual childhood," in which she showed how even the insignificant details of everyday life can provide all the opportunity necessary for spiritual growth. Her last months were marked by the debilitating pain of tuberculosis and an interior trial of faith that continued to the end. All this she offered to Jesus as an act of love which asked for nothing but the capacity to keep loving. "Living on Love," written when she had just received the first indications of her impending death and had been asked to begin work on her autobiography, conveys the full ardor of her soul. This passage (verses 1–3, 5–9, and 15) is from *The Poetry of St. Thérèse of Lisieux,* tr. Donald Kenney, o.c.d. (ICS Publications, 1995), which has the full poem in French as well as in English translation.

THOMAS À KEMPIS
"The Wonderful Effect of Divine Love," p. 124
"Lord That Giveth Strength," p. 196
"Four Things That Bring Much Inward Peace," p. 199
The Imitation of Christ has probably inspired more Christians than any other spiritual work except the Bible. In a simple, confident style, it gives the essence of what is necessary to follow in the footsteps of Jesus. Its traditional author, Thomas à Kempis (c. 1380–1471), spent most of his life in Holland among the Brethren of the Common Life, a community devoted to a life of simplicity, selfless service, and the imitation of Christ in tumultuous times that fostered other notable European mystics, including Saint Catherine of Siena, Heinrich Suso, and Nicholas of Cusa. "The Wonderful Effect of Divine Love" (from book 3, chapter 5) stands at the heart of the *Imitation,* where the tone shifts from practical counsels on spiritual effort to an intimate dialogue between the yearning soul and the fulfilling Spirit. "Lord That Giveth Strength" is from book 3, chapter 10; "Four Things That

Bring Much Inward Peace," from book 3, chapter 23. This translation, based on that of Anthony Hoskins (c. 1613), is from *Of the Imitation of Christ: Four Books by Thomas à Kempis* (Oxford, 1903: The World's Classics, vol. 49).

THE TORAH
"The Shema," p. 103

Drawn mostly from injunctions in the Torah, the five books of Moses that begin the Jewish scriptures, the Shema has been recited since Biblical times as the central affirmation of the Jewish faith. (The name comes from the first word: *sh'ma*, "Hear!") Tradition prescribes that the Shema be spoken with entire concentration of heart and mind. As the fundamental prayer of Judaism it is repeated three times a day by many, and many more hope to have it upon their lips at the time of death. Its significance for Christians as well is enshrined in the Gospels. Translated for this book by Ellen Lehmann Beeler.

TUKARAM
"In Me Thou Livest," p. 72
"When I Lose Myself in Thee," p. 73
"The One Thing Needed," p. 208
"Think on His Name," p. 218

A Hindu mystic of seventeenth-century India, Tukaram (c. 1598–1650) started out in life as a prosperous peasant farmer and grain seller. A series of devastating personal losses plunged him into a despair so deep it completely purged his worldly aspirations. Turning all his thoughts to God, he began to express his longings in devotional songs of compelling simplicity and beauty – songs that became lyrics of joy when he reached illumination and dedicated his life to teaching the common people to aspire to God-realization. His thousands of compositions in the vernacular are considered the foundation of Marathi literature. He is regarded as an important representative of the Bhakti school of Hindu mysticism, the way of devotion. From John S. Hoyland, *An Indian Peasant Mystic: Translations from Tukaram* (Allenson & Co., 1932).

UPANISHADS

"Invocations to the Upanishads," pp. 29, 101, 177

The Upanishads are a collection of inspired dialogues, poetry, and visionary exposition appended to the Vedas, India's ancient scriptures, which date back to at least 1500 B.C.E.; how long they were preserved before that in India's long oral tradition can only be conjectured. The oldest mystical documents in the world, they remain to this day the purest expressions of the perennial philosophy: the conviction that underlying the phenomenal world is a changeless reality with which any human being can be united consciously through an inner search following disciplines that have been taught in every age and culture. The invocations in this book are associated with various Upanishads, often with more than one. The passages on p. 101 were translated for meditation by Eknath Easwaran; the others are from *The Upanishads: Breath of the Eternal,* tr. Swami Prabhavananda and Frederick Manchester (Vedanta Press, 1968). See also RIG VEDA and particular Upanishads: AMRITABINDU, CHANDOGYA, ISHA, KATHA, KENA, TEJOBINDU, SHVETASHVATARA.

YELLOW LARK, CHIEF

"Let Me Walk in Beauty," p. 188

A famous prayer by Chief Yellow Lark, a nineteenth-century medicine man of the Lakota Sioux.

YOGA VASISHTHA

"The Lamp of Wisdom," p. 235

A selection (3:23–30) from the Yoga Vasishtha, a Hindu scripture in the form of a dialogue in which the questions of young prince Rama, a divine incarnation of Vishnu, are answered by his spiritual teacher, the sage Vasishtha. This is a free rendering for meditation by Eknath Easwaran.

Glossary

atman [Sanskrit "self"] The Self, the immanent aspect of the Godhead, the divine essence in every creature.

bodhi [Sanskrit, from *buddh,* "to wake up"] Illumination, realization of the unity of life.

Brahma [Sanskrit] God the Creator.

Brahman [Sanskrit] The Supreme Reality underlying life; the divine ground of existence; the transcendent, impersonal Godhead.

brahmin [Sanskrit, "one worthy of knowing Brahman"] In traditional Hindu society, a member of the priestly or learned caste.

chakora [Hindi] A mythical bird.

dharana [Sanskrit] In classical yoga, the first stage of meditation, in which concentration deepens until the senses close down and physical consciousness is transcended. See also *dhyana.*

dharma [Pali *dhamma*; from Sanskrit *dhri,* "to support"] Truth, righteousness, law; duty; justice; virtue; the nature or essential quality or peculiar condition of anything; the universal spiritual Law that holds all things together in a unity; in Buddhism, the Buddha's teaching as a whole.

dhyana [Sanskrit] Meditation; unbroken concentration; the second stage of meditation in classical yoga. See also *dharana* and *samadhi.*

guna [Sanskrit] Quality; specifically, one of the three qualities which make up the phenomenal world: *sattva,* law or virtue; *rajas,* energy or passion; *tamas,* inertia or ignorance.

guru [Sanskrit "heavy"] A spiritual teacher.

Kaaba [Arabic *Ka'ba*] A small stone building in the court of the Great Mosque in Mecca; the sacred center of the Islamic world, toward which Muslims turn when praying.

karma [from Sanskrit *kri,* "to do"] Action; something "done" in thought or word as well as action; former actions which will lead to certain results in a cause and effect relationship.

kundalini [Sanskrit, "coiled power"] The evolutionary energy drawn on for spiritual progress, awakened through meditation.

mantram [Sanskrit; also *mantra*] A spiritual formula; a holy name or phrase inherently connected with the reality it represents, often repeated for the purpose of stilling the mind – a practice found in all major traditions of mysticism.

maya [Sanskrit] The hypnotic illusion of duality; appearance, as contrasted with divine Reality; the illusion of separateness that gives rise to suffering and sorrow.

Mussalman [Persian & Urdu *Musulman*] A Muslim.

nirvana [from Sanskrit *nir*, "out," and *vana*, "to blow"] The extinction of separateness and realization of the unity of life.

Om The cosmic sound, heard in deep meditation; a sacred syllable signifying Brahman or the Godhead, uttered at the beginning and end of Hindu prayers.

samadhi [Sanskrit] A state of intense concentration in which consciousness is completely unified and the sense of duality between knower and known disappears; the third and final stage of meditation in classical yoga.

shanti [Sanskrit] Peace, tranquility, complete stillness of mind, "the peace that passeth understanding" (often repeated three times at the end of a Hindu prayer as a benediction).

Shiva God in the aspect of destroyer, presiding over the destruction of separate consciousness (thus granting illumination) and of death itself.

Sufi [Arabic] An Islamic mystic; perhaps from *suf*, the Arabic word for wool, in reference to the garments of early Muslim ascetics.

Sufism The mystic tradition in Islam.

Vishnu [Sanskrit "all-pervading"] In Hinduism, God as Preserver, whose incarnations on earth include Rama and Krishna.

Vrindavan [Sanskrit *Vrindavana*] The boyhood village of Krishna, a divine incarnation.

yoga [from Sanskrit *yuj*, "to unite"] Union with Reality, Self-realization; a systematic path or set of practices for attaining this state; as a proper noun, the system of meditation taught by Patanjali [c. 200 B.C.E.] and described in his *Yoga Sutras*.

yogi [Sanskrit] One who practices yoga.

Acknowledgments

Special thanks to friends who contributed translations in other anthologies:

Stephen H. Ruppenthal, whose translations for this book are now included in his *Path of Direct Awakening* (Berkeley Hills, 2003)

Mary Ford-Grabowsky, for the translation of Hildegard of Bingen (p. 165) from her collection *Prayers for All People* (Doubleday, 1995)

We are also grateful to the following translators and publishers, whose copyright statements below extend the copyright page of this book:

Fakhruddin Araqi, "The Shining Essence" (p. 50): From Jonathan Star, *The Inner Treasure: An Introduction to the World's Sacred and Mystical Writings* (New York: J. P. Tarcher / Putnam), p. 132. Copyright 1999 by Jonathan Star.

Saint Anselm, "Teach Me" (p. 54): From *The Fire and the Cloud: An Anthology of Catholic Spirituality*, edited by the Rev. David A. Fleming, S.M. Copyright 1978 by Paulist Press, New York.

Dov Baer of Mezhirech, "You Must Forget Yourself in Prayer" (p. 61): Excerpt from *Your Word Is Fire,* © 1993 Arthur Green and Barry W. Holtz (Woodstock, VT: Jewish Lights Publishing). $14.95 + $3.75 s/h. Order by mail or call 800 962 4544 or online at www.jewishlights.com. Permission granted by Jewish Lights Publishing, P.O. Box 237, Woodstock, VT 05091.

Elizabeth of the Trinity, "O My God, Trinity Whom I Adore" (p. 115): From *The Complete Works of Elizabeth of the Trinity* translated by Sr. Aletheia Kane, O.C.D. Copyright 1984 by Washington Province of Discalced Carmelites, ICS Publications, 2131 Lincoln Road N.E., Washington, DC 20002-1199, USA, www.icspublications.org.

Mahatma Gandhi, "The Path" (p. 202) & "In the Midst of Darkness" (p. 203): From *My Religion,* by M. K Gandhi. Copyright 1955 by Navajivan Trust, Ahmedabad, India; "Self-Surrender" (p. 248): From *From Yeravda*

Mandir: Ashram Observances, by M. K. Gandhi. Copyright 1935 by Navajivan Trust.

Rabbi Abraham Isaac Kook, "Radiant Is the World Soul" (p. 39): From *Abraham Isaac Kook,* translated by Ben Zion Bokser. Copyright 1978 by Paulist Press, New York.

Baba Kuhi of Shiraz, "Only God I Saw" (p. 77): From Reynold A. Nicholson, *The Mystics of Islam* (G. Bell & Sons, 1914). Copyright Reynold A. Nicholson, 1914.

Sri Ramakrishna, "Songs of Sri Ramakrishna" (pp. 69, 113, 114, 222, 231): From *The Gospel of Sri Ramakrishna,* as translated into English by Swami Nikhilananda and published by the Ramakrishna-Vivekananda Center of New York. Copyright 1942 by Swami Nikhilananda.

Rig Veda, "United in Heart" (p. 102) & The Chandi, "Hymn to the Divine Mother" (p. 36): From *Prayers and Meditations Compiled from the Scriptures of India,* edited by Swami Prabhavananda and Clive Johnson. Copyright 1967 by Vedanta Press, Hollywood, California.

Jalaluddin Rumi, "A Garden beyond Paradise" (p. 246): From *A Garden beyond Paradise: The Mystical Poetry of Rumi,* edited by Jonathan Star and Shahram Shiva (Bantam Books, 1992).

Sri Sarada Devi, "The Whole World Is Your Own" (p.147): From *Holy Mother* by Swami Nikhilananda, published by the Ramakrishna-Vivekananda Center of New York, Copyright 1962 by Swami Nikhilananda.

Mahmud Shabestari, "The Mirror of This World" (p. 38): From Jonathan Star, *The Inner Treasure: An Introduction to the World's Sacred and Mystical Writings* (New York: J. P. Tarcher/Putnam), p. 137. Copyright 1999 by Jonathan Star.

Saint Thérèse of Lisieux, "Living on Love" (p. 162): From *The Poetry of St. Thérèse of Lisieux* translated by Donald Kinney, o.c.d. Copyright 1995 by Washington Province of Discalced Carmelites, ICS Publications, 2131 Lincoln Road N.E., Washington, DC 20002-1199, USA, www.icspublications.org.

The Upanishads, "Invocations" (pp. 29, 177): From *The Upanishads: Breath of the Eternal,* translated by Swami Prabhavananda and Frederick Manchester (Hollywood: Vedanta Press, 1968).

Other sources and translators are mentioned in the notes.

Index by Author & Source

Amritabindu Upanishad, 84
Ansari of Herat, 131
Anselm, Saint, 54
Araqi, Fakhruddin, 50
Augustine, Saint, 230
Azikri, Rabbi Eleazar, 123
Baba Kuhi of Shiraz, 77
Bahya ibn Pakuda, Rabbi, 154
Bernard of Clairvaux, Saint, 204
Bhagavad Gita, 74, 110, 166, 182,
    189, 210, 241
Book of Common Prayer, 179
Buddha: see Dhammapada;
    Sutta Nipata
Catherine of Genoa, Saint, 226
Chaitanya, Sri, 220
Chandi, 36
Chandogya Upanishad, 49, 224,
    244
Clare of Assisi, Saint, 93
Dhammapada, 78, 86, 142, 183,
    236
Dov Baer of Mezhirech, 61
Eckhart, Meister, 79
Eknath Easwaran, 253
Elizabeth of the Trinity, 115
Francis de Sales, Saint, 122, 207
Francis of Assisi, Saint, 109

Gabirol, Solomon Ibn, 67, 185
Gandhi, Mahatma, 202, 203, 248
Gospel of Saint Matthew, 106
Hasan Kaimi Baba, 158
Hildegard of Bingen, 165
Ignatius of Loyola, Saint, 129
Inayat Khan, Hazrat, 96, 97, 139
Isaiah, 146
Isha Upanishad, 31
Jalaluddin Rumi, 246
Jewish Liturgy, 83, 128, 184
John the Elder, 119
Kabir, 40, 168, 169, 170, 221, 234
Katha Upanishad, 62, 80, 212,
    227
Kena Upanishad, 56
Kook, Abraham Isaac, Rabbi, 39
Lao Tzu, 34, 35, 141, 145
Law, William, 48
Lawrence, Brother, 152
Matthew, Saint, Gospel of, 106
Mechthild of Magdeburg, 119
Meera, 116, 117, 118, 215, 216, 217
Mehta, Narsinha, 148
Mishkat al-Masabih, 181
Native American Tradition, 186
Newman, John Henry,
    Cardinal, 130

Omkar, Swami, 138
Pakuda, Bahya ibn, Rabbi, 154
Ortha nan Gaidheal, 150, 151
Paramananda, Swami, 45, 46, 47
Patrick, Saint, 149
Paul, Saint, 140
Psalm 23, 201
Psalm 24, 89
Psalm 100, 30
Psalm 139, 52
Rabi'a, 120, 121
Ramakrishna, Sri, Songs of, 69, 113, 114, 222, 231
Ramdas, Swami, 37, 94, 95, 157, 171, 219
Ravidas, 249
Rig Veda, 102, 178
Rumi, Jalaluddin, 246
Sarada Devi, Sri, 147
Seng Ts'an, 58
Shabestari, Mahmud, 38
Shankara, 209, 223

Shantideva, 68
Shvetashvatara Upanishad, 42, 90, 159, 192, 232, 250
Sivananda, Swami, 55, 144
Sutta Nipata, 104, 200
Symeon the New Theologian, Saint, 60
Tejobindu Upanishad, 70
Teresa of Avila, Saint, 156, 172, 173, 206
Thérèse of Lisieux, Saint, 162
Thomas à Kempis, 124, 196, 199
Torah, 103
Tukaram, 72, 73, 208, 218
Upanishads, Invocations, 29, 101, 177;
    Amritabindu, 84;
    Chandogya, 49, 224, 244;
    Isha, 31;
    Katha, 62, 80, 212, 227;
    Kena, 56
Yellow Lark, Chief, 188
Yoga Vasishtha, 235

Index by Title & First Line

A

166 A leaf, a flower, a fruit
185 *Adon Olam*
138 Adorable presence
124 Ah, Lord God, thou holy lover of my soul
182 *All Paths Lead to Me*
86 All that we are is the result of what we have thought
68 As a blind man feels when he finds a pearl
183 As an archer aims his arrow
224 As by knowing one lump of clay, dear one
40 As oil is in the oil seed
117 As the lotus dies without water

B

241 *Be Aware of Me Always*
54 Be it mine to look up to thy light
58 *Believing in Mind*
123 *Beloved of the Soul*
141 *The Best*
106 Blessed are the poor in spirit
183 *The Blessing of a Well-Trained Mind*

67 Bow down before God, my precious thinking soul
159 Brahman, attributeless Reality
236 *The Brahmin*
34 Break into the peace within
250 *The Bridge to Immortality*

C

95 *The Central Truth*
220 Chant the Name of the Lord and his glory
222 *Chant the Sweet Name of God*
149 *Christ Be with Me*
156 Christ has no body now on earth but yours
244 *The City of Brahman*
249 *The City of God*
117 *Come, Beloved*
236 Cross the river bravely

D

121 *Dawn Prayer*
130 Dear Jesus, help us to spread your fragrance
253 Dear Lord, please fill my heart with love and devotion

48 *The Deepest Part of Thy Soul*

104 *Discourse on Good Will*

113 *Dive Deep, O Mind*

37 *Divine Mystery*

207 *Do Not Look with Fear*

154 *Duties of the Heart*

69 *Dwell, O Mind, within Yourself*

E

89 *The Earth Is the Lord's*

230 *Entering into Joy*

140 *Epistle on Love*

210 *The Eternal Godhead*

216 *Even with Your Last Breath*

128 *Evening Prayer for the Sabbath*

38 Every particle of the world is a mirror

246 Everything you see has its roots in the unseen world

F

29 Filled with Brahman are the things we see

145 *Finding Unity*

200 For those struggling in midstream

95 Forget not the central truth

199 *Four Things That Bring Much Inward Peace*

234 *The Fruit of the Tree*

G

246 *A Garden beyond Paradise*

142 *Give Up Anger*

178 *God Makes the Rivers to Flow*

186 *Great Life-Giving Spirit*

186 Great Spirit of love, come to me

249 Grieve Not is the name of my town

H

78 He has completed his voyage

171 *He Is Omnipresent*

182 He who knows me as his own divine Self

103 Hear, O Israel

173 *Her Heart Is Full of Joy*

159 *Hidden in the Heart*

34 *Holding to the Constant*

116 How am I to come to you

219 *How Great Is His Name!*

36 *Hymn to the Divine Mother*

I

169 I am a citizen of that kingdom

179 *I Am the Resurrection & the Life*

122 *I Am Thine, Lord*

181 *I Come to Him Running*

203 I do dimly perceive that whilst everything around me

223 I do not ask Thee, Mother

172 *I Gave All My Heart*

165 I, God, am in your midst

114 *I Have Joined My Heart to Thee*

60 *I Know That He Reveals Himself*

202 I know the path: it is strait and narrow

50 I look into the mirror and see my own beauty
60 I sit alone, apart from all the world
147 I tell you one thing
150 I weave a silence onto my lips
221 I weave your name on the loom of my mind
144 If anyone speaks ill of you
140 If I speak in the tongues of men and of angels
215 If you want to know the power
219 If you would have peace
74 *The Illumined Man*
230 Imagine if all the tumult of the body were to quiet down
212 *The Immortal*
72 *In Me Thou Livest*
171 In my heart I found my Beloved
244 In the city of Brahman is a secret dwelling
77 In the market, in the cloister – only God I saw
203 *In the Midst of Darkness*
131 In the name of God
80 In the secret cave of the heart
128 In this moment of silent communion with Thee
165 *In Your Midst*
31 *The Inner Ruler*
131 *Invocations* (Ansari)
29, 101, 177 *Invocations* (Upanishads)
200 *The Island*

J

129 *Just Because You Are My God*

K

97 *Khatum*

L

235 *The Lamp of Wisdom*
177 Lead me from the unreal to the real
188 *Let Me Walk in Beauty*
206 *Let Nothing Upset You*
70 Let us meditate on the shining Self
118 *Life of My Life*
67 *The Living God*
162 *Living on Love*
168 The Lord is in me
201 *The Lord Is My Shepherd*
119 *Lord, I Bring Thee My Treasure*
109 Lord, make me an instrument of thy peace
90 *The Lord of Life*
196 *Lord That Giveth Strength*
52 *Lord, Thou Hast Searched Me*
232 *Love the Lord and Be Free*

M

104 May all beings be filled with joy and peace
184 May His great Name grow exalted
29 May quietness descend upon my limbs
177 May my speech be one with my mind

101 May the Lord of Love protect us

101 May the Lord of Day grant us peace

192 May the Lord of Love, who projects himself

149 May the strength of God pilot me

102 May we be united in heart

90 May we harness body and mind

68 *The Miracle of Illumination*

93 *The Mirror of Eternity*

38 *The Mirror of This World*

35 *Mother of All Things*

184 *Mourner's Kaddish*

196 My child, I am the Lord, that giveth strength

199 My child, now will I teach thee

120 My God and my Lord

N

84 *The Nectar of Immortality*

120 *Night Prayer*

234 No longer am I the man I used to be

O

55 O adorable Lord of mercy and love

121 O God, the night has passed and the day has dawned

188 O Great Spirit, whose voice I hear in the winds

46 *O Infinite Being!*

52 O Lord, Thou hast searched me

37 O Mother Divine

152 O my God, since thou art with me

115 *O My God, Trinity Whom I Adore*

220 *O Name, Stream Down in Moonlight*

158 O seeker of truth, it is your heart's eye you must open

170 O seeker, the simple union is the best

47 O Supreme Deity, Mother of the moving

45 O Thou compassionate All-loving Spirit

96 O Thou, the Almighty Sun

36 O thou the giver of all blessings

97 O Thou, who art the Perfection of Love

110 Of those who love you as the Lord of Love

208 Of what avail this restless, hurrying activity

129 Oh, my God, I want to love you

231 Oh, when will dawn for me that day of blessedness

162 On the evening of love, speaking without parable

192 *The One Appearing as Many*

208 *The One Thing Needed*

79 *One With God*

83 Only for God doth my soul wait in stillness

77 *Only God I Saw*

47 *Origin of All*

248 Our existence as embodied beings is purely momentary

P

202 *The Path*

158 *The Path of Love*

116 *The Path to Your Dwelling*

62 *Perennial Joy*

93 Place your mind before the mirror of eternity

215 *The Power of the Holy Name*

152 *The Practice of the Presence of God*

139 *Prayer for Peace* (Hazrat Inayat Khan)

138 *Prayer for Peace* (Swami Omkar)

96 *Prayer for the Peace of the World*

109 *The Prayer of Saint Francis*

R

39 *Radiant Is the World Soul*

30 Raise a shout for the Lord

80 *The Razor's Edge*

148 *The Real Lovers of God*

42 *The River of God*

169 *The River of Love*

S

83 *Sabbath Prayer*

78 *The Saint*

126 *A Sea of Peace*

248 *Self-Surrender*

139 Send us Thy peace, O Lord

106 *The Sermon on the Mount*

253 *Setu Prayer*

204 She is truly like a star

103 *The Shema*

130 *Shine through Us*

50 *The Shining Essence*

70 *The Shining Self*

150 *Silence*

170 *Simple Union*

217 *Singing Your Name*

209 *Soul of My Soul*

45 *Source of Our Existence*

42 Spiritual aspirants ask their teacher

94 *Such Is a Saint!*

T

72 Take, Lord, unto Thyself

54 *Teach Me*

74 Tell me of the man who lives in wisdom

40 *The Temple of the Lord*

56 *That Invisible One*

204 *That Wondrous Star*

141 The best, like water

58 The great Way has no impediments

62 The joy of the spirit ever abides

250 The learned say life is self-created

31 The Lord is enshrined in the hearts of all

168 The Lord is in me, the Lord is in you

201 The Lord is my shepherd; I shall not want

185 The Lord of the universe

84 The mind may be said to be of two kinds

181 The Prophet said: *God most high has said*

189 The Self dwells in the house of the body

56 The student inquires: "Who makes my mind think?"

35 The universe had a beginning

146 Then, when you call, the Lord will answer

212 There is a city with eleven gates

148 They are the real lovers of God

218 *Think on His Name*

49 *This Is the Self*

151 This morning, as I kindle the fire on my hearth

151 *This Morning I Pray*

49 This universe comes forth from Brahman

241 Those who are free from selfish attachments

145 Those who know do not speak

210 Those who remember me at the time of death

231 *Thou One without a Second*

48 Though God be everywhere present

223 *Thy Holy Name*

235 To all who long and strive to realize the Self

232 To know the unity of all life

227 *The Tree of Eternity*

86 *Twin Verses*

U

102 *United in Heart*

55 *Universal Prayer*

157 *Unshakable Faith*

168 *The Unstruck Bells and Drums*

W

110 *The Way of Love*

144 *The Way to Peace*

221 *Weaving Your Name*

154 What is meant by wholehearted devotion

189 *What Is Real Never Ceases*

166 *Whatever You Do*

73 *When I Lose Myself in Thee*

226 When the good God calls us in this world

94 When the heart burns at the sufferings of others

73 When thus I lose myself in Thee, my God

146 *When You Call*

218 Whilst thou art busy at work

79 Whoever has God in mind

147 *The Whole World Is Your Own*

222 With beaming face chant the sweet name of God

177 With our ears may we hear what is good

124 *The Wonderful Effect of Divine Love*

30 *Worship the Lord in Gladness*

Y

156 *You Are Christ's Hands*

224 *You Are That*

118 You are the light of my life

209 You are the soul of my soul

61 *You Must Forget Yourself in Prayer*

119 You who are hidden and concealed within me